RESOURCE BOOKS FOR TEACHERS

series editor

ALAN MALEY

D1411067

BEGINNERS

Peter Grundy

Oxford University Press

OXFORD

UNIVERSITY PRESS

Great Clarendon Street, Oxford OX2 6DP

Oxford University Press is a department of the University of Oxford.
It furthers the University's objective of excellence in research, scholarship,
and education by publishing worldwide in

Oxford New York

Auckland Cape Town Dar es Salaam Hong Kong Karachi
Kuala Lumpur Madrid Melbourne Mexico City Nairobi
New Delhi Shanghai Taipei Toronto

With offices in

Argentina Austria Brazil Chile Czech Republic France Greece
Guatemala Hungary Italy Japan Poland Portugal Singapore
South Korea Switzerland Thailand Turkey Ukraine Vietnam

OXFORD and OXFORD ENGLISH are registered trade marks of
Oxford University Press in the UK and in certain other countries

ISBN: 978 0 19 437200 8

Typeset by Wyvern Typesetting, Bristol, UK

Printed in China

Acknowledgements

One of the most exciting things about teaching beginners is the feeling that one is learning more than they are. I vividly remember several groups who taught me more than I taught them. In particular, I benefited from working with Judith Baker on a beginners' course at Pilgrims some years ago. Since then, Judith and I have shared many beginners ideas and together discussed what a book like this should contain. I had hoped to work more closely with her on the book itself, but unfortunately it was not to be. She remains a silent partner in this endeavour.

I also owe a great deal to two former MA students at Durham. One is Ian White, whose perceptive dissertation on handwriting planted a seed. His influence is acknowledged more fully at the beginning of Chapter 5. The other is Anna Korea, whose deep understanding of beginners, and particularly child beginners, was an inspiration to me. I have included some of her ideas in this book.

There are several others to whom I am indebted, including British Council Summer School colleagues and participants at Durham, particularly Melanie Ellis, Printha Ellis, John Morgan, Valentine Philip, and Valentina Toocheva, who all made valuable suggestions on drafts of parts of this book which I gratefully acted on. I have also gratefully accepted ideas from a number of others, who are acknowledged in the body of the book.

Finally, I owe a great deal to Alan Maley, series editor of Resource Books for Teachers, and to the English Language Teaching division of OUP, and in particular to Cristina Whitecross, Anne Conybeare, Julia Sallabank, and an anonymous reader. Alan, Cristina, and Anne gave me the confidence to pursue this project and helped me to translate it into a better book than it would otherwise have been. Julia's extremely acute comments on the various drafts and meticulous desk editing turned a whimsical manuscript into the book you are reading now. The remaining faults are mine.

Contents

3 Basics

4 Language basics

8 Games

9 Interactions

The author and series editor

Peter Grundy has taught in schools in Britain and Germany, has worked in higher education as a teacher trainer, and from 1979 to 2002 was a lecturer at the University of Durham, where he taught applied and theoretical linguistics to undergraduates and postgraduates and English for Academic Purposes to the University's overseas students. He has had considerable experience of language teaching and teacher training on summer schools and seminars in Britain and overseas stretching back over more than twenty years. He is currently Associate Principal Lecturer at Northumbria University. He is the author of *Newspapers*, in this series (OUP 1993), as well as *Doing Pragmatics*, *Writing for Study Purposes* (with Arthur Brookes), and *Language through Literature* (with Susan Bassnett).

Alan Maley worked for The British Council from 1962 to 1988, serving as English Language Officer in Yugoslavia, Ghana, Italy, France, and China, and as Regional Representative for The British Council in South India (Madras). From 1988 to 1993 he was Director-General of the Bell Educational Trust, Cambridge. From 1993 to 1998 he was Senior Fellow in the Department of English Language and Literature of the National University of Singapore. From 1998 to 2002 he was Director of the Graduate Programme at Assumption University, Bangkok. He is now a freelance consultant. He has written *Literature*, in this series (with Alan Duff, OUP 1990), *Beyond Words*, *Sounds Interesting*, *Sounds Intriguing*, *Words*, *Variations on a Theme*, and *Drama Techniques in Language Learning* (all with Alan Duff), *The Mind's Eye* (with Françoise Grellet and Alan Duff), *Learning to Listen* and *Poem into Poem* (with Sandra Moulding), and *Short and Sweet*.

Foreword

All too often beginners are lumped together under the misleading epithet 'false beginners'. This book dismantles the twin myths which underlie this categorization.

The first of these is the convenient belief that there are no 'real' beginners any more. (Convenient because it allows us to get on with 'exciting' activities with learners, who can be presumed already to be in control of the basics.) This book confronts us with the awkward fact that there are still substantial numbers of real beginners, with problems of a quite different order from those experienced even by 'false' beginners.

The second myth is the belief that 'beginners' are a single category. In his acute and helpful analysis, Peter Grundy shows just how many different groups of beginners there are, each requiring subtly different approaches.

A constant problem with older beginners is the discrepancy between their relatively high levels of affective and cognitive development, and their low level of linguistic competence in the target language. This book is notably successful in showing how activities requiring very limited language can none the less be made cognitively and affectively challenging. In this way, beginning learners are enabled to bring their adult experiences to bear on the language they imperfectly command, without the loss of self-esteem and the sense of hopelessness which low-level materials all too often provoke.

There is a proper understanding of the very real and stubborn difficulties faced by beginners, especially when a new script is also involved. Chapter 5, 'Roman script', is a rare instance of a serious attempt to deal with this set of problems.

The book succeeds in being simultaneously innovative and realistic. It combines the best of communicative practice with the pragmatic realization that beginners cannot be expected to run before they have learnt to walk. In this it seems to me to have mastered 'the art of doing ordinary things extraordinarily well'.

In my view, this book makes a significant contribution to a hitherto neglected area of professional concern.

Alan Maley

Introduction

What is a beginner?

This is a book for teachers of beginners and near-beginners. But what is a beginner?

This question could obviously be answered in many different ways. One fashionable answer is to claim that there is no such thing as an absolute beginner of English. Thanks to the status of English as a world language, it is frequently claimed that everyone is aware of isolated lexical items ('President', 'jeans'), set phrases ('made in Korea'), and sentences ('We shall overcome'), and that everyone has a relatively developed idea of English phonology.

For these reasons, teacher trainers in Britain frequently begin training sessions on teaching beginners with the claim that there are no real beginners of English. Trainees are asked if they know Italian, and when they say no, are asked to reflect for a moment on just how much Italian they really do know. If we all know 'spaghetti', 'pizza', and a hundred other Italian words, the argument runs, how much more English will our supposed beginners actually know?

On the other hand, it would be hard to maintain this happy illusion if you found yourself, as I did recently, in front of a class of beginners from various countries of the world. The class included several students who appeared to have no English whatsoever and no knowledge of the Roman alphabet either. My task seemed still more difficult when I discovered that two were illiterate in their mother tongues, and that another was so taken aback to find that she had a male teacher that she refused to give any vocal indication of her presence. The only abstract representations we appeared to share were Arabic numerals and a few internationally-known symbols and logos. So much for the claim that there is no such thing as an adult beginner of English!

Because the term 'beginner' has such a range of connotations, it is often helpful to think in terms of categories of beginner.

Several of these categories are discussed below.

The absolute beginner

Described as a 'pre-beginner' by Earl Stevick, this rare species is not yet extinct. How to proceed with such a learner?

It obviously helps to be able to speak the learner's language or to have someone available to translate. In the very first stages, pictures, board drawings, and realia will obviously be crucial. They enable the learner to understand a meaning before hearing the linguistic representation. One really useful technique with absolute beginners is 'doubling', where the teacher speaks for the beginner (perhaps speaking over the beginner's shoulder) and the beginner then appropriates the model.

Reflection Think for a moment of a language where you would be an absolute beginner. Imagine you were about to have your first lesson. How would you feel? What would you be thinking? Do you think an absolute English beginner would have the same feelings or different ones?

The false beginner

This term covers a much wider range of competences than is sometimes recognized. Some false beginners have received no formal instruction, others may be self-taught, others have experienced at least some classroom teaching. All are likely to experience what we might call 'recognition syndrome': they will recognize, half-way through an exercise, that they do in fact know more than they (and the teacher) were assuming. The problem is that this knowledge is not always accurate. Other false beginners retain formulaic expressions. Most false beginners have strongly developed attitudes to the language and culture. These may be very positive (for example, where the language knowledge reflects popular culture) or relatively negative (for example, where the language knowledge is the remnant of a previous unsuccessful learning experience).

Reflection Think of a language where you would be a false beginner. What is the extent of your previous knowledge and how did you acquire it? Do you think that a false English beginner's experience would be like yours? In what ways might it be similar or different?

The beginner with/without second language learning experience

If a beginner has already had a second language learning experience, this will colour their expectations of a further second language learning experience. Items from an established second language may also be transferred to the new second language, particularly when the two languages share common or similar linguistic items. Thus a student may be a 'first time' beginner (a beginner both as a language learner and as a learner of English), or the student may be an 'experienced' beginner who has already had a second language learning experience. Where both kinds of beginner are found in the same classroom, each will be making different kinds of discovery and undergoing different kinds of experience.

Reflection If you have learnt more than one second language, think for a moment of all the ways in which your later experience of learning a language was affected by your earlier one(s). Which of these effects made the second learning experience easier and which made it more difficult?

The adult beginner

The adult beginner will always have some clear reason for wanting to learn a language. It may be recreational or occupational, and it is important for the teacher to identify this reason. Frequently, the language taught will need to be orientated towards this goal, even in the earliest stages. Adult English beginners often strongly believe that they are still beginners at their age because they are not good learners. Other adult beginners will have ideas about how they learn best and how successful they are likely to be. They are often mistaken in these views, but teachers ignore them at their peril. In particular, a teacher needs to decide how much use to make of written forms for beginners who do not know the Roman alphabet—this decision will depend partly on how reliant the learners are on written forms as a learning aid.

Reflection Have you ever been an adult beginner? How relevant to your experience is the description above? What other aspects of being an adult beginnner were important in your case?

The young beginner

It is useful to think through the effects of at least the following factors on your young beginners:

Age Are your learners so young that linguistic explanation would be fruitless for this reason alone? Or have your beginners reached the age at which they will consciously employ cognitive skills to help them learn?

Learning culture Are your learners accustomed to working out of school hours? If so, how hard do they work? Is this equally true for boys and girls? Are they likely to employ their own favoured methods (such as rote learning) whatever other strategies they experience in the classroom? Or do they regard the end of school as the end of work for the day?

Motivation Are they enthusiastic about learning English? Do they see any use for it? Has English got parental support? How will this motivation feed on success and survive setbacks?

Maturity Are your learners at an age when risk-taking, making errors, and any consequential loss of face is particularly unwelcome? Are they especially self-conscious, or inclined to discuss certain topics only in closed groups? Are they especially critical of what they see as irrelevant materials or unsympathetic teaching styles?

Learning context Are you the only teacher of English that your learners are working with, or are they also learning English from another source? What are their attitudes to the different contexts in which they are learning?

Teacher role Will they learn because they are enthusiastic, no matter who teaches them and how they are taught? Or will you have to teach them all that they are to learn in the face of their intention to make as little progress as possible?

Reflection Do you recall how your age and attitudes, and the context in which you learnt a language as a young beginner, affected how you learnt? Try to focus on one or two particular moments in your language learning experience that might have been different if you had been other than a young beginner.

The evening class beginner

Evening class beginners are invariably adults who have been hard at work all day (like the teacher). There is very often a wide ability range in adult beginners classes. This can result in a group developing mutual support strategies, but more often it causes stresses and frustrations within the group. Evening classes sometimes attract oddballs.

Evening class beginners are usually more enthusiastic at the outset than later, when they realize the real work involved in learning a language. Different members of a group will (be able to) devote very different amounts of time to homework and out-of-class learning. Evening classes typically experience erratic absenteeism and high drop-out rates.

All this means that evening classes are a special challenge for the teacher of beginners, who will need to develop well thought out strategies to manage these problems.

Reflection If you were ever an evening class language learner, what strategies might (a) you and (b) your teacher have adopted to make your experience more successful? What made you give up your evening class? If you have never been an evening class language learner, why not?

Beginning English as a school subject

Teachers of English as a school subject typically have little freedom to depart from the prescribed syllabus. School learners may be more interested in passing written exams than in learning to use the language. Beginners may find themselves particularly reliant on a coursebook precisely because English is being taught as a knowledge-rich subject rather than as a language for use. For this reason, the supplementary ideas in a book like this need to be particularly carefully dovetailed with the coursebook. Sometimes an idea may be used as a preparation for the coursebook unit, sometimes as a reinforcement.

Reflection Do you recall how your teachers balanced coursebook work with supplementary materials when you were a beginner? How comfortable were you with the balance your teacher struck? Is there any difference between the way you felt about this at the time and the way you feel about it now?

Intensive courses for beginners

Intensive courses have many advantages: for example, progress is rapid and tangible. A group also gets used to working together and rapidly develops intra-group support systems. The teacher's engagement is entirely with one group rather than being dissipated among several groups—this obviously gives the teacher more opportunity to think hard about the individual needs of the learners and the progress of the group as a whole. Often, too, teacher and students establish out-of-hours social contact under such conditions.

Reflection Think back to your own early stage second language learning experience. How would it have been different if it had been more intensive? What can you learn from this about teaching beginners even when working on the three classes per week, drip-feed system?

The overseas beginner

Learning a language as a visitor in the country where it is spoken is a very different experience from learning it in your own country. For one thing, the classroom is only one of many learning situations. To take an apparently trivial example which symbolizes this difference, in an English-speaking country a non-English surname will probably sound exotic and the visitor will frequently be asked to spell their name aloud.

Some visitors find the new culture an invigorating stimulus to language learning. For others, the host culture appears unfamiliar and threatening, and self-confidence rapidly ebbs away. Research studies sometimes show surprising things: for example, Svanes has shown that a slightly critical attitude to the host culture can be associated with more successful language learning. Learners' attitudes to the host culture also vary over time, and this variation affects their motivation. If you are teaching beginners who have recently arrived in an English-speaking country, you will need to give real attention to their attitudes to the host culture.

Reflection Think of a country in which you would be a beginner. Imagine how living there might affect you as a language learner.

The beginner's existing knowledge

At present there is considerable interest amongst applied linguists in the effects of 'prior knowledge', or knowledge of the first language, on second language acquisition. Of course, learners are not usually aware of the extent to which this prior knowledge affects the route or rate of second language acquisition. Teachers, though, do need to be aware of some of the research, and can benefit enormously in terms of both professional development and knowledge about second language acquisition even from reading a single volume of collected papers such as Gass and Schachter's (relatively challenging) *Linguistic Perspectives on Second Language Acquisition*.

If you know, for example, that a learner's mother tongue has fewer relative structures than English or even no relatives at all, then you will expect avoidance of the relative structures that are not found in the mother tongue. It is obviously important to know what will be difficult for any particular learner because their mother tongue parameter setting does not coincide with that of the target language.

Reflection Think of a language of which you have been a relatively successful learner. If English is not your first language, this will do well. Can you think of a number of ways in which your knowledge of the your mother tongue influenced what you learnt and how you learnt it? Try to think both of influences of which you were aware at the time and influences that you might be able to identify now that you know more about the similarities and differences between the two languages.

Beginning to speak

We have probably all had the experience of learning to say who we are in the first ten minutes of our encounter with a foreign language. And we have probably all had tens of hours of exposure to a foreign language without making any attempt to speak it ourselves. In the first case, of course, we were being taught in a classroom, and in the second we were not. Although as learners we have the expectation that we should speak immediately, there are a number of points that might be made that question this assumption:

- A long 'silent period' occurs before we begin to speak our mother tongue. During this period, we presumably learn a great deal about the syntax and phonology of the language. Could this be an important factor in successful language acquisition?
- If we try to speak right at the beginning, we are bound to transfer our mother tongue phonology, and this may quickly become established as the second language phonology.
- Because it is extremely difficult to achieve native speaker-like phonology in a second language, learners naturally concentrate on the mechanical difficulties of pronunciation in the early stages when arguably they should be listening for meaning. And when they concentrate on mechanical difficulties, the students tend to learn *about* the language rather than the language itself.

The teacher of beginners therefore has a difficult balance to strike between listening for meaning activities on the one hand and listening as a preparation for speaking on the other.

A second issue worth considering is Krashen's claim that input, rather than output opportunity, is the only necessary condition for successful second language acquisition. Theoretically, according to Krashen, one could acquire a second language without ever exercising productive skills. If this is right, speaking is not essential to successful learning although it may be very useful. (Indeed, wanting to be able to speak a second language will usually be the first reason for learning it.)

Reflection Can you recall your own first attempts to speak a second language? Were they voluntary or forced? What was the relationship between listening and speaking? What aspects of phonology did you concentrate on? Are there any features of your attitude to speaking at an early stage that still affect you when you speak a second language?

Beginning to write

There are several points to make about early stage writing:

- As is well known, in English sound–spelling correspondences are only consistent up to a point. This means that learners have problems going from speaking to writing. They also have

problems, which frequently affect intelligibility, going from written texts to speaking. The sooner a learner recognizes that the written system of English is an unreliable guide to its spoken form, the easier the teacher's task.
- Traditionally, most early stage writing activities take the form of copying-type exercises.
- There are real-world needs for writing, and the products of these needs are authentic text-types. Every teacher has to decide whether, or to what extent, to practise writing in ways that do not reflect these real-world needs and which are likely to lead to products that are not authentic.
- Different categories of beginner will have different attitudes to writing. The case of adult learners has already been mentioned. Another category is the student who knows from the outset that proficiency will be measured largely or entirely by ability to write.

Reflection Can you recall to what extent your early stage writing in a second language was directed by your teacher or self-determined? Did your teacher use writing more to teach language or more to teach the writing process by focusing, even in the early stages, on areas like planning and organization of material, awareness of readership, and rewriting?

The beginner without Roman alphabet

This is actually a wider category than it might at first sight seem to be. The learner may be illiterate, or literate but familiar only with an ideographic writing system (such as Chinese) or a non-Roman alphabet (such as Greek or Arabic). Even being illiterate is a relatively broad category which includes learners able to recognize and understand varying amounts of written text as well as learners with varying degrees of manual dexterity and varying degrees of familiarity with writing implements. In a similar way, some literate beginners without Roman alphabet have never attempted to write from left to right. Each of these categories of beginner requires individualized attention and practice with the specialized materials available.

Reflection Think for a minute of the problems you would be likely to have as an early stage learner of a language with an unfamiliar writing system. What would you be expecting your teacher to do to help you?

Language distance

Beginners are very quick to make assumptions about the 'distance' between the language they are learning and their mother tongue. Language distance may be measured at various linguistic levels: syntactic, phonological, pragmatic, etc. Very frequently a learner's conscious perception of language distance may be inaccurate because it rests on a linguistic feature which is particularly salient to the learner. For example, English and French share many common lexical items but have very different phonologies. The phonological difficulties learners experience when moving from one of these languages to the other may result from their making only a partially accurate assumption about language distance based on a recognition of shared lexical items. Areas of particular salience which beginners use to compute language distance include

- phonetic segments that are close to those in their mother tongue
- phonetic segments that are not found in their mother tongue
- presence or absence of tone and intonation
- shared lexical items
- presence or absence of inflection in the two languages
- word order
- politeness phenomena and forms of address
- writing systems (ideographic, alphabetic, etc.)
- affective and aesthetic aspects of the target language.

Strictly speaking, a factor like the writing system has nothing to do with language distance and we need therefore to distinguish between the effects on language learning of the learner's perception of language distance, and the effects of actual language distance. Language distance and perceptions of language distance are important because they will determine the extent to which a learner transfers mother-tongue features to the target language.

Reflection Think of the foreign languages you know. Based on your intuitive feelings, can you rank them in terms of distance from your mother tongue? What factors do you take into account in reaching this ranking? Next, try to think of real criteria for establishing language distance and use these criteria to rank your languages. Does your ranking remain the same?

Learning strategies

Anyone who has seriously tried to learn a second language knows how much time it takes and how it requires a real reorganization of lifestyle. As beginners make these changes in their routines, they inevitably think about learning strategies. They may have broad strategies concerning, for example, the opportunities they seek out for learning, as well as very particular strategies, for example, whether to ration the use of a dictionary. In between, there will be a whole range of strategies based on beliefs about learning. These strategies will change as the learners grow more experienced.

Gradually learners become aware of strategies and of the importance of what Ellis and Sinclair call 'learning to learn'. It certainly helps if a teacher can think through and suggest useful learning strategies to beginners as well as encourage them to employ their own self-discovered strategies in effective ways over relevant language areas. Similarly, a style of teaching which allows learners to observe and learn from each other extends the individual's awareness of strategy and study skill options.

Reflection List three or four strategies you used when you were learning a foreign language. Do you think these strategies would be useful to other learners? What other strategies might you use if you tried to learn a new language now?

The categories of beginner and outlines of attitude above are necessarily general. As teachers of beginners, we also need to take into account the considerable variety of individual differences in attitude that may be present in a single classroom. There are likely to be students suffering from all kinds of anxieties about teaching method, about their own aptitude and performance, about learning generally, about cultural understanding, and about their ability to interact with fellow students and their teacher. These anxieties tend to be greater among beginners than other learners, precisely because the target language is still mysterious. At the other end of the scale, many beginners have unrealistic expectations about their likely progress. Still others may be regarding their opportunity to learn English as a heaven-sent opportunity, even a luxury.

Because of this variety of categories of beginner and of individual attitudes, the ideas that you will find in this book are designed to allow each member of the group to take part in a class activity and to take away from the activity what is most important for their own learning. This means that each activity promotes individual language learning in a whole class context.

How to use this book

Each chapter in this book (except Chapter 1) contains a number of activities which you can use to supplement your coursebook. The way they are sequenced varies from chapter to chapter. In Chapter 2, for example, the order reflects the extent to which the teacher models the language to be learnt. They can, of course, be used in any order. Similarly, you can use activities from any chapter according to your (or your students') needs or interests.

Chapter 1 encourages you to reflect on the language syllabus and your approach to teaching beginners. The approach which is advocated is that which underlies the activities in the rest of the book.

In Chapter 2, there are a number of activities which are suitable for learners with no knowledge of the Roman alphabet. These are labelled 'NRA' ('non-Roman alphabet') under 'Level'.

Level

Although this is a book for teachers of beginners, it would be of limited use if it only provided ideas for the very first lessons. For that reason, the activities are designed for the first hundred hours of instruction, and are graded as follows:

Level 1 = 0–25 hours   Level 3 = 51–75 hours
Level 2 = 26–50 hours   Level 4 = 76–100 hours

Each activity is set out in a 'recipe' format, following the standard practice of this series. This means that there are step-by-step instructions for you to work from. Because of the complications of instruction giving discussed in Chapter 1 (see page 23, 'Decision 7: Giving instructions'), I have not tried to explain in detail how to convey these instructions to your students. You will therefore need to think carefully about how to do this, especially if you do not speak their mother tongue or are teaching a non-homogeneous group.

The language structure or function which is likely to occur is always indicated—this will make it easier for you to integrate these activities with your coursebook.

The Index at the end of the book lists the activities by language area and topic, and is intended as a quick reference to help you choose an activity relevant to your students. It also lists those activities which are suitable for younger learners.

1 Decisions

I remember my first foreign language learning lesson as if it were yesterday. In fact, it was in 1953. It was also the first time I was kept in after school—until a quarter to five in fact, by which time I had learnt:

If I see 'is' or 'are' or 'do' or 'does'
I must use some sense,
I don't translate
But simply use the present tense.

Although my first foreign language lesson was conducted entirely in my mother tongue, it was to be four years before I understood it. Now, of course, I know that it was an exemplary demonstration of the grammar-translation method.

Many years later, I enjoyed my first German lesson as an adult beginner at a German language school. Some months later, when my German teacher and I had become good friends, I was cheeky enough to suggest that 'Hier ist eine Karte; das ist eine Karte von Europa' was a slightly uninspiring first sentence and not immediately useful in the bar across the road from the language school. 'Yes,' she said, 'I had the same feeling about my first English sentence.' 'Here's a map; it's a map of Europe'? I suggested apprehensively. 'No,' she replied. 'Mr Macdonald is a hunter.'

This is a book for teachers of beginners who are looking for simple, practical, enjoyable activities that can be used either alongside or even in place of coursebooks. There are two emphases to every activity. The first is that it should be genuinely communicative, in the sense that every learner gives voice to a meaning that is important to them. And the second is that it should promote the effective use of some structure or function. This second emphasis recognizes the need many teachers, and perhaps learners too, feel for being able to put a name to what is being learnt. In a strange way, this emphasis is a cousin, a very distant cousin, of my first language lesson. The first emphasis, too, bears some family resemblance to the first German sentence I learnt, except that in this book the activities focus on genuinely interesting and useful language.

Decision 1: Syllabus options

Task 1 Before reading further, take a few minutes to think about the three questions below. Each question is followed by a

continuous line—decide where you position yourself on this
continuum and mark the line accordingly:

1 When you think about your work as a teacher, are you more
guided by syllabus content or method and approach?

| syllabus content | ├─────────────────────────────────┤ | method and approach |

2 When you think of the language a learner is to acquire, do you
think more of its formal properties (structures and lexis) or of its
functional properties (how it is actually used in speech acts)?

| formal properties | ├─────────────────────────────────┤ | functional properties |

3 Do you think a language syllabus should be described in terms
of product (what is to be learnt) or process (how the learner is to
work)?

| product-orientated | ├─────────────────────────────────┤ | process-orientated |

These are major issues on which the syllabus designer for
beginners has to take decisions. In the next two sections, we will
examine in more detail the issue of whether the syllabus should
be spelt out in terms of content, as is traditional, and whether a
product-orientated or a process-orientated approach is more
effective.

Decision 2: Content or method

Syllabus content may be thought of as structural, with
grammatical structures (tenses, etc.), vocabulary, and
phonological structures (phonemes, phonotactic processes,
suprasegmental intonation patterns, etc.) being graded for
difficulty and specified for each stage in the learning process. Or
it may be thought of as notional, as in Van Ek's 'Threshold level
for European language learners', where the syllabus is spelt out
in terms of notions such as location, possibility, etc. Or the
syllabus may be thought of as functional, as in many
contemporary coursebooks where students learn how to greet,
express opinions, admire, and disagree.

An alternative to the content-based syllabus is to define the
syllabus in terms of methodology and approach. There are, for
example, methods or approaches appropriate to the structurally

graded syllabus referred to above. An approach that has attracted
a lot of attention in recent years is the procedural or task-based
approach. Here, each activity is thought of firstly as a task or
sub-task requiring completion strategies, and only secondly as a
vehicle for practising language. In the task-based approach, the
language required will inevitably be more difficult to specify and
control. A task-based approach is half-way between the purely
subject-centred approach implied by a structural syllabus and a
truly learner-centred approach in which the syllabus designer or
teacher thinks first of the learner and of questions such as

– how do learners acquire language?
– what language does the learner need?
– what will interest the learner as a person?

Some years ago now, Judith Baker of Pilgrims and I team-taught
an intensive beginners group. We decided to work entirely in a
learner-centred way and adapted an evangelical Christian tract
which asked its readers to consider their 'uniqueness'. We used
the cardinal principles of this tract as criteria against which to
judge any activity we were contemplating using, so that every
activity had to address at least one of the following:

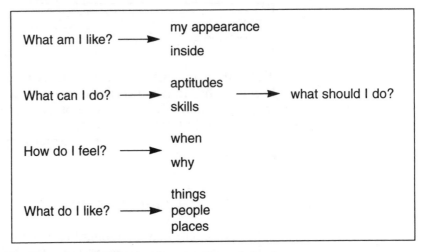

In following these criteria, we allowed the language content to
take care of itself and instead concentrated primarily on the
personal relevance of our activities and materials. In doing this,
we were asking the same question as Candlin when he asks
'whether it is possible to separate so easily what we have been
calling content from what we have been calling method or
procedure' (Candlin 1984: 32).

Decision 3: Product or process

If one thinks of a syllabus as a graded sequence of items to be
taught, one inevitably finds oneself focusing on the product of

learning, since the syllabus is in effect a list of the outcomes or products of successful language teaching. The traditional approach to language teaching has been to begin a lesson by 'presenting' part of this product to learners. Then, through a series of activities, usually listening, followed by controlled practice, followed by freer practice, the learners are taken to the stage when the product is considered learnt. Yet when one thinks about this, it seems illogical to *begin* by presenting the product or outcome of successful learning. Logic would surely suggest that it is the learning process itself where the focus should be.

It is much easier to grasp this point if one thinks of a concrete example: take writing an essay. The product-orientated approach begins by presenting a model to learners, which, after some analysis, they attempt to imitate. The focus is on the essay or product. In contrast, the process-orientated approach practises the processes involved in finding and defining the topic of the essay, including organizing the materials and deciding which points will be given prominence, struggling to find the words to express the meaning most exactly, considering how the arguments will need to be framed to work on the reader, and the difficult processes of rewriting, both editing and proof-reading. The focus here is on the *writing* or process.

As you work through the activities in this book, you will see that the focus is not on syllabus content and product only, as in traditional approaches, but also very frequently and perhaps predominantly on approach and on process. Although the language to be practised is specified in each activity, the focus will typically be on the learning process, and the approach will typically take into account the personal interests of individual learners.

Decision 4: Teaching strategies for beginners

Take a few minutes to work through the two tasks below.

Task 2 What proportion of language at the beginner level do you believe should be taught in class, and what proportion should be learnt outside class? Mark each of the following categories of beginner at the appropriate point on the continuum:

1 the absolute beginner
2 the false beginner
3 the adult beginner
4 the young beginner
5 the first time beginner
6 the experienced beginner
7 the evening class beginner
8 the school subject beginner
9 the intensive course beginner
10 the beginner without Roman alphabet

(For example, if you believed that adult beginners should learn 99 per cent of their English in class, you would write '3' at the very left-hand end of the line.)

100% class learning		100% out of class learning

Task 3 Imagine that the box beside each type of beginner in the diagram below represents the total class time available. What proportion of this time should be spent on whole class work (C), on small group work (G), on pair work (P), and on individual work (I)? Divide the space up into four sections according to your opinion. For example, if you divided up the space next to 'Absolute beginner' like this:

Absolute beginner	C	G	P	I

you would be showing that you thought most time should be spent on whole class work, next most on group work, rather less on pair work, and almost none working individually.

Absolute beginner	
False beginner	
Adult beginner	
Experienced beginner	
Evening class beginner	
School beginner	
Intensive beginner	
No Roman alphabet	

The purpose of Tasks 2 and 3 is to make us think hard about the different ways in which elements of a beginners' course will need to be combined for different types of learners (absolute/false, child/adult) and types of class (intensive/evening/school subject). All too often we resolve these issues intuitively rather than by thinking our policy through carefully at the outset and adjusting it continuously in response to the changing needs of our students.

Decision 5: Classroom activities

The chapters that follow contain activities geared to different stages and elements in the early learning process and to different types of learner. Below you will find a list of some of the topics and activities that are covered in subsequent chapters.

Task 4 As you read through this list, tick each topic or idea which you have used with beginners. Think for a moment about what you did and how successful it was:

Getting started

Building on existing knowledge	Using gesture

Basics

Numbers	Future forms
Helping students to talk about themselves	*Have got*
	The alphabet
Colours	Making questions
Telling the time	Pronunciation
Days of the week	Stress
To be	Roman script
Perfect forms	Teaching vocabulary
Progressive forms	Making dictionaries

Experiences

Mime	Readers
Autobiography	Newspapers
Traveller's tales	Group presentations
Letters	Listening comprehension
Tests	Video
Questionnaires	CALL
Surveys	Games
Reading comprehension	Using realia

Towards autonomy

Making questions	Peripheral learning
Describing people	Learner scrapbooks
Describing the street	Learner diaries
Teaching speech acts	Translation
Eavesdropping	Teaching learning strategies
Using native speakers	Self-instruction

Decision 6: Introducing supplementary materials

Until now it has been taken for granted that we all want to use supplementary materials with our beginners. But do teachers of beginners generally use supplementary materials?

Task 5 The question below invites you to consider the extent to which you use such resources in your own teaching. Again, mark the continuous line at the appropriate point:

When you last taught beginners, what proportion of your work was coursebook based and what proportion made use of supplementary materials?

Whether you do use supplementary materials or rely largely or exclusively on your coursebook will be partly a matter of convenience (How much time do you have available?), partly a matter of the type of beginner you work with (What are your students' expectations?), partly a matter of institutional policy (To what extent are you free to innovate?), and partly, and perhaps most importantly, a matter of your methodological stance—are you a product-orientated, graded-sequence teacher?

If there were the time, and the students had the appropriate expectations, and we had the freedom to innovate, then we would almost certainly want to use supplementary materials with our beginners. One purpose of this book is to solve the time problem by providing ready-made supplementary activities. And if you begin as you mean to continue, with supplementary materials, you will readily solve the student expectations question. The freedom or otherwise to innovate is usually a matter of institutional policy—I hope this book will help you show the decision-makers in your institution that innovation is worthwhile when it introduces authentic materials, practises authentic skills, and promotes self-study.

But consider for a moment the methodological issue raised at the end of the paragraph before last. If you were to evaluate the activities in this book by the graded-sequence criterion, then because they cannot readily be graded in relation to each other, they would obviously score very low. But imagine taking a different, less traditional methodological position. Imagine your syllabus approach was the one that Judith Baker and I followed (described on page 18), and complete the task below:

Task 6 Turn back for a moment to page 18 and re-read the boxed set of criteria we worked with. Now reach for the coursebook you are using at present and turn to any unit in the book. Work through the unit considering each exercise against our criteria. How many exercises actually survive?

If, as is likely, very few do, and if you are persuaded that a learner-centred, process-orientated methodology is really more appropriate, then you could consider a more radical alternative. You might try replacing the coursebook with the kind of activities that you will find in this book. You can even supplement these with the kind of ideas you will think of for yourself as you recognize the needs and interests of your own students.

Decision 7: Giving instructions

We can readily distinguish two very different functions of classroom language. Most of the language we use is made available to our students in the expectation that it will be acquired. But a significant proportion has a different, 'metalingual', function—we use it to give instructions and to explain meanings and forms.

I am not going to say anything about the use of language to explain meanings and forms, except that this book never advocates it, since we all acquired our first languages entirely, or virtually entirely, without metalingual assistance. But giving instructions is a different matter. Unless our students can understand what is required, they cannot undertake the task intended. Coursebooks tend to solve this problem by using a restricted set of headings which are frequently repeated. 'Practice exercise 1', although not expressed as an instruction, is a typical example of the kind of heading our students would understand as one.

In a resource book of this kind where we want our learners to do a whole range of original things, instruction giving becomes very important and much more problematical. Teachers of beginners are rather like swimming teachers—the instructions are unusually important. And if being a good teacher is partly a matter of making it possible for students to learn for themselves, then the instructions we give on each occasion when we set this process off will be one measure of how good we are at our job.

Task 7 Rank the following methods of giving instructions to beginners in the order in which you make use of them in your own teaching:

- by speaking English
- through written English
- by speaking the students' mother tongue
- through written mother-tongue text
- through mime
- by using pictures
- by drawing
- with realia
- by example
- by modelling the required response
- through an interpreter
- through higher-level students
- by relying on some students to understand and explain to the others.

My guess is that you regarded each of these techniques as separate (which in fact I encouraged you to do in the way I set the task), and were thinking of using one for one type of activity and another for another.

Task 8 Now turn to the very first activity at the beginning of the next chapter, 'What I already know in English' (page 25), and imagine yourself doing it with a new group of beginners. Imagine the way the lesson would be likely to go. Now return to the list of instruction giving techniques above, and think again about how you would use them in this activity.

The reality is, of course, that you would have used nearly all of these methods of giving instructions, and probably two or three less obvious strategies that were not in the list at all.

2 First lessons

This chapter contains ten first lesson ideas. Several are also suitable for lessons other than the very first one, and some can be used a number of times, often with small variations. Most are suited to non-Roman alphabet (NRA) learners or can be adapted for them—where this is the case, it is indicated. A continuation lesson is also suggested for each activity. Finally, the activities are ordered, with those which have the least teacher modelling of language at the beginning of the chapter and those which have the most at the end.

2.1 What I already know in English

LEVEL   1; adults and older children; adaptable for NRA

TIME   50 minutes

LANGUAGE   I like [spaghetti] and [volleyball]

PROCEDURE   1 Ask the students to write down all the words they can think of in their mother tongue that they think English has borrowed. Give one or two examples, such as 'spaghetti' (Italian), 'chow mein' (Cantonese), or 'sugar' (Arabic).

2 Ask each student to write down all the words they think their mother tongue has borrowed from English. Give an example, such as 'volleyball' (more or less universal).

3 Ask the students to compare their lists with each other and add any further examples that fellow students have written down and they did not have. While they are doing this, go round checking to make sure that the words are spelt correctly.

4 When the lists are complete, use mime and paralinguistic signals to convey the meaning of 'I like'. Ask each student to tick all the items on their lists that they like.

5 Each student should tell the class about three items they like using the formula 'I like [item] and [item] and [item]'. Encourage mime accompaniment.

CONTINUATION   This activity leads naturally to one student telling another what a
third student likes.

VARIATION   You can also ask each student to write down all the words that
they think occur in both English and their mother tongue but
which both languages have borrowed from elsewhere. For non-
Greek speakers 'telephone' will probably be a good example, or
for non-Arabic speakers 'algebra'.

COMMENTS   In this activity the students have to think hard about their own
language and culture in order to make guesses about English.
This is good fun. Most students enjoy discovering that they are
frequently wrong and are occasionally thrilled to discover they
are right.

2.2 What I already know about English-speaking culture

LEVEL   1–2; older children

TIME   45 minutes

LANGUAGE   **Titles of English films and books, and explanations and
translations in the mother tongue**

PROCEDURE   1 Ask each member of the class to make lists of

– all the films they have seen with English titles
– all the books they have read with English titles
– all the pop groups they know of with English names
– all the television series they watch with English names.

2 Ask the students to write either a translation into their mother
tongue or an explanation in English or their mother tongue after
each item on their list. For example, most beginners could
translate *Jurassic Park* into their mother tongue but might prefer
to say (in their mother tongue) that *Terminator 2* was the second
film about a robot sent to earth to destroy human life.

CONTINUATION   Once past the very first stage, this activity can be returned to.
This time, ask the students to make an evaluative comment such
as 'I thought . . . was boring' or 'I enjoyed . . . very much'.

2.3 This is Big Ben

LEVEL	1–2; children and adults; NRA
TIME	30 minutes
MATERIALS	One sheet of A3 paper for each student
LANGUAGE	Phrases that name well-known buildings such as 'This is the White House', 'This is Big Ben', 'This is Buckingham Palace'
PROCEDURE	1 Distribute one sheet of A3 paper to each student and ask them to draw all the buildings they know in an English-speaking city of their choice. Encourage the students to construct a collage or superimpose one building on another so as to achieve an aesthetic effect. Do the same yourself.
	2 Ask the students to work in small groups and tell each other the names of the buildings they have drawn, using phrases beginning with 'This is . . .' Demonstrate with your own drawings.
	3 Tell the students to write the names of the buildings on their drawings and, if you wish, display the drawings on the walls.
CONTINUATION	This activity leads naturally to saying who lives and/or what happens in the buildings.
VARIATION 1	This activity can be made simpler by allowing the students to draw buildings from all the English-speaking cities they know or by supplying picture prompts of well-known buildings.
VARIATION 2	You can base this activity on drawing people engaging in various sports.
COMMENTS	This activity establishes an important principle for the first stages of learning English: that the students will often associate language with pictures or images.

2.4 Beginning with geography

LEVEL	1; children and adults; NRA
TIME	40 minutes
MATERIALS	One sheet of A3 paper for each student, map of the world
LANGUAGE	Names of countries

PROCEDURE

1 This activity may be done individually or in small groups. Give each student/group a sheet of A3 paper and tell them to draw the countries whose names you will say in the appropriate place on the sheet of paper. Begin by saying the name of an English-speaking country and then allow time for each student to draw it. Continue with English-speaking countries until five or six have been drawn and then pause for the students to check that they have not made any mistakes. Ask what the countries have in common.

2 When you resume, choose a set of countries that have some other common feature. For example, countries that are on the Equator, or oil-producing countries, or, in a multinational class, all the countries that the different students come from. Again, pause after dictating five or six and, as in Step 1, check for mistakes and ask what the countries have in common.

3 Continue until you judge the students have had enough.

4 Finally, ask the students to write the countries' English names on their maps (in their own script if necessary) and display the maps on the wall alongside a map of the world.

CONTINUATION

This leads naturally to doing the activity the other way round. Say 'English-speaking countries' and the students draw in and name five. Repeat with 'oil-producing countries', etc.

VARIATION

Ask the students to draw maps of Britain (or another English-speaking country). Dictate a list of towns (perhaps using the football league table which you will find in virtually all English-language newspapers printed in non-English-speaking countries). The students mark each team's location on the map. To simplify this task, prepare and distribute maps with the names of principal cities marked in. There are lots of categories you can use besides football teams. For example, the locations of the head offices or manufacturing bases of major companies for business English students, places members of the class have visited, places you have lived in yourself, etc. This activity leads naturally to making simple sentences about these towns which describe their size, what sorts of places they are, what industry is associated with them, etc.

COMMENTS

1 This activity combines the problems of knowing where a country is and what it looks like with learning its English name. If you choose countries carefully, recognizing the English name will be the easiest part of the activity.

2 The longer this activity goes on, the more difficult it gets to draw the map, as the students discover they have not got the scale right or positioned countries appropriately.

2.5 Everyone can choose a first lesson

LEVEL   1–4; small groups of adults; NRA

TIME   20 minutes per lesson

MATERIALS   Several pictures, one supplied by each student

LANGUAGE   Descriptions, dialogues, etc. as determined by the teacher

PREPARATION   1 Ask each student to choose a magazine picture which they
would like to explore through English. Explain that the picture
may be of two or more people having a conversation, or it may
be any indoor or outdoor scene. These pictures should be
brought to class the day before the first English lesson. Display
them on the wall in the order in which you decide to work with
them.

2 Construct a lesson around the first picture. This may mean
writing a very simple dialogue, inventing a guessing game where
the students have to decide which vocabulary item represents
each object in the picture, choosing names for the people in the
picture, describing how people dress, what they do, etc.

PROCEDURE   Teach the lesson you have prepared around the picture chosen
by the student.

CONTINUATION   As each student's picture is used, encourage them to choose a
replacement picture which then goes to the end of the queue. As
students see how you use the pictures, they will begin to choose
replacements which reflect areas of English they want to learn
more about. They can even add in writing an indication of what
they hope might be taught with their picture.

COMMENTS   1 It is often a good idea to try and arrange the lesson so that it
ends with a wall display which incorporates the picture.

2 Because this provides a series of 'first lessons', it takes some of
the apprehension out of beginning to learn a language. And
because the students all get a turn at choosing their first lesson,
they are able to decide whose lesson is best without thinking that
the teacher is to blame for less exciting lessons.

2.6 I spy, we spy . . .

LEVEL	1–4; children (and adults); NRA
TIME	30 minutes
MATERIALS	Small pieces of paper or card; blu-tack for Variation
LANGUAGE	Single words such as table, chair, wall, floor, ceiling

PROCEDURE

1 Choose an object in the classroom and say its name in English, for example, 'desk'. As you say 'desk', look hard at it, and when the students also stare at it, indicate that the word 'desk' refers to the object the students are staring at.

2 Choose a second object and say its name, but this time the students must decide what object is being referred to and stare at it themselves. As students identify the right object by direction of gaze, indicate by nodding that they are correct.

3 Repeat Step 2 with several new objects. From time to time repeat familiar words already identified.

4 Move to a Total Physical Response (TPR) type activity by saying 'Look at the desk', 'Look at the ceiling', etc.

5 Step 4 can now be extended with instructions like 'Sit on the desk', 'Touch the wall', etc.

CONTINUATION

This vocabulary accumulation task can be used whenever you move to a new environment, for example, when you look through the window, go outside, or go into a shop. As the students acquire vocabulary of their own, they can take turns at saying words too, while their classmates indicate their understanding by directing their gaze at the right object.

VARIATION

Instead of moving to the TPR activity at Step 4, ask the students either (a) to draw a labelled picture of the objects in their classroom or (b) to write the names of the classroom objects on small pieces of paper or card and move round blu-tacking these labels to the appropriate objects.

COMMENTS

1 This activity helps to prevent learners from translating by giving them an image and an English word to associate with it rather than asking them to associate an English and a mother-tongue word. And it does it in a fun way.

2 Total Physical Response is a teaching method in which students associate language with movement by obeying, giving, and describing instructions to carry out various actions. Although there is an obvious TPR follow-on as suggested in Steps 4 and 5, it is not necessary to move to this stage at all.

3 This activity also introduces the fundamental technique of indicating understanding by non-linguistic means.

2.7 Individualized learning

LEVEL	1–4; adults; NRA
TIME	10 minutes per learner + practice time
MATERIALS	Cassette recorder and tape for each learner
LANGUAGE	What the learners want to say about their reasons for learning English and about themselves
CLASS SIZE	This method is ideal for one-to-one teaching. It will not work in classes of more than eight students or when the teacher does not speak the students' language
PREPARATION	Make sure that each student has a portable cassette recorder and a blank tape.
PROCEDURE	1 Work with each student in turn. (While you are doing this, make sure that the students who are waiting for you to come to them have something useful to do, such as preparing their sentences or revising previous work.) Ask the student to say two or three brief sentences in their mother tongue about why they want to learn English. Record this on the individual student's cassette recorder and immediately afterwards record your own translation into English.
	2 Allow each student plenty of time to listen to and practise saying these, their own, first English sentences. Offer help with pronunciation as required.
CONTINUATION	Once this way of learning is accepted by the student(s), you can provide regular updates of the tape, including consecutive translations of the language the student wants to learn (for example, ways of introducing him- or herself, etc.) or descriptions of the student's property or contents of handbag or wallet (for example, 'This is my front door key, this key . . .' etc.).
VARIATION 1	You can also ask the students to record their mother-tongue sentences for homework, and you can record the English-language equivalents out of class too. This helps to avoid frustration in class while you are giving all your attention to a single student.
VARIATION 2	Instead of asking the students to say why they want to learn English at Step 1, ask them to talk about their interests, their work, their families, or their special needs, etc.

COMMENTS

1 This is a Community Language Learning technique in that the teacher acts as the provider of only the language that the learners indicate they require. Here it is individualized so that each learner can use it outside the context of the language learning classroom (or 'community').

2 If you establish Variation 1 as a way of working, each student will be able to use this way of learning to the extent that suits her or him.

Acknowledgement

Hou Xu of Southeast University, Nanjing, suggested asking the students to talk about their interests and needs in the first class.

2.8 Signs and language

LEVEL

1; children and adults; NRA

TIME

30 minutes

LANGUAGE

Words that can be represented by gesture

PROCEDURE

1 Begin by nodding your head and then saying 'yes'. Then shake your head and say 'no'. Get the class to do the same.

2 Indicate (upturned palms, looking from side to side at the students) that you want someone in the class to produce a gesture. When someone does, give the English word. Get the class to use the gesture and say the English word. If no one offers a gesture, point at yourself and say 'I'm', then imitate drinking and say 'drinking'. Appeal again for someone to produce a gesture. This time you will almost certainly be successful.

3 Continue until you have 10–15 words which everyone can say and associate with a gesture.

COMMENTS

1 This is an easy way to start English because gestures come naturally. Moreover, the words are easy to remember when they come accompanied by a gesture.

2 Right from the outset, you establish that the students can ask for a word by miming.

3 You should aim to incorporate these first words into the lessons that follow. Often your beginners will continue to use them with gestures (and a degree of humour) for some weeks.

Acknowledgement

This idea first occurred to me while I was working with a British Sign Language Diploma group at Durham and the students were explaining how they taught BSL beginners.

2.9 Provenance and status

LEVEL

1; best with adults from various countries; adaptable for NRA

TIME

60 minutes

MATERIALS

Large sheets of paper (such as A3); an atlas is useful

LANGUAGE

(Following on from learning names and introducing self) I'm from [place]; I'm married/single; I've got [number] children

PROCEDURE

1 Distribute an A3 sheet to each learner and ask the students to write 'I'm [name]' (as already learnt) wherever they choose on the sheet. Do the same thing yourself on the board.

2 Draw a rough map of your own country on the board (leaving room for other information) and mark the town where you live. For example:

Indicate to the students that they should draw their own countries on their sheets and mark their own home towns.

3 Tell the class about yourself in the following way: 'I'm [name]. I'm from [home town]'. So, for example, I would say, 'I'm Peter. I'm from Durham'. Ask each of the students to tell the class who they are and where they are from using the same structure.

4 Tell the students to write 'I'm from [home town]' under their maps.

5 Draw a picture of your family status on the board. Even if you 'can't draw', you can do a representation like the following:

Tell the class about yourself in the following way (I use my own case as an example): 'I'm Peter. I'm from Durham. I'm married (indicating wedding ring). I've got two children (indicating children on the board).'

6 Ask the students to draw their families on their A3 sheets. Each student should tell the class about their family status. You may have to supply vocabulary and prompt now and again.

7 Tell the students to write a description of their family status under the drawings of their families.

CONTINUATION

1 This activity leads naturally to asking the students their names, where they are from, and if they are married; and then getting them to ask each other. Once you get to questions, be sure to draw the students' attention to the difference between

I'm from Durham (/frəm/), and
Where are you from? (/frɒm/)

This helps to reinforce the important point that written English does not provide a reliable guide to the pronunciation of spoken English.

2 The large sheets of paper can also be used for follow-up lessons in which the students learn to describe themselves, their likes and dislikes, and their regular habits.

2.10 This is who we are

LEVEL
1; children and adults; smaller classes

TIME
30 minutes for smaller classes

MATERIALS
Photocopies of seating plans (see Preparation); calendar (optional); pictures of faces (for Variation)

LANGUAGE
Ways of giving information about oneself, including 'I'm . . .', 'My birthday's on . . .', etc.

PREPARATION
1 Prepare a seating plan for the class but in such a way that everyone is represented by an outline. For example, ten students sitting round a table might look like this:

2 Make a photocopy of the seating plan for each student.

PROCEDURE
1 Distribute a copy of the seating plan to each student. Say your name using the formula 'I'm . . .'. Ask each student to say their name. Their classmates should write each name in the appropriate outline.

2 Tell the class when your birthday is using the formula 'My birthday's on . . .'. A calendar can be a useful aid at this stage. Ask each student to say when their birthday is. Their classmates should add this information to the outline.

CONTINUATION
Continue with other categories of information if you wish. These might include occupation, family status, place of abode, hobbies.

VARIATION   A particularly good variation for one-to-one teaching is to work with an empty face outline such as the one below:

You can find a picture of someone who looks a bit like your student, white out the facial features, and then photocopy it. Or your student may be able to supply you with a passport photograph which you can enlarge and doctor. All sorts of information can be written in, and new outlines can be supplied as students learn to say more about themselves.

3 Basics

This chapter contains fifteen activities to help you to teach numbers, time, and colour in the first stages of learning English. Although this chapter is called 'Basics', it is important to recognize that many of the things in this chapter are not as straightforward as they at first seem to be. For example, although one of the first things we learn in a foreign language is how to count, it is also one of the last things we fully master.

One frequently hears stories in Britain about non-native speaker doctors who take a patient's temperature and read the thermometer in their mother tongue, thereby destroying with three or four words all the confidence so laboriously built up until that moment. Or take the problems associated with colours: the set of colour terms that exist in one language will never be in a one-to-one relationship with the colour terms in another. This makes it very difficult for a language learner to use colour terms in a second language in the way that a native speaker would. And even native speakers have problems with determining colour—try walking down a street and deciding whether cars are blue, green, grey, or silver and you will see what I mean.

Quite often 'Basics' can be taught through existing rhymes such as

Thirty days have September,
April, June, and November.
All the rest have thirty-one,
Excepting February alone,
Which has twenty-eight days clear
And twenty-nine in each leap year.

One, two, three, four, five,
Once I caught a fish alive;
Six, seven, eight, nine, ten,
Then I let him go again.
Why did you let him go?
Because he bit my finger so.
Which finger did he bite?
This little finger on the right.

and 'Solomon Grundy', which I sometimes make into a guessing game by setting it out like this:

SG   (Solomon Grundy)
BoM   (Born on Monday)
ChoT   (Christened on Tuesday)

MoW	(Married on Wednesday)
TioTh	(Took ill on Thursday)
WoF	(Worse on Friday)
DoS	(Died on Saturday)
BoS	(Buried on Sunday)
AtwteoSG	(And that was the end of Solomon Grundy)

One thing you will not find in this chapter are ideas for
non-linguistic responses to language. These are nevertheless very
important in the language classroom. There are some well-known
games of this sort, such as 'Simon Says', where the students
react differently to each utterance depending on whether or not it
is preceded by 'Simon says . . .'. Nodding, winking, standing
up, raising a hand, etc. are all simple ways students can use for
signalling understanding (or sometimes lack of it). Similarly, one
can construct activities like, 'If you are male/female, left-/right-
handed etc., do x' to test understanding. These TPR-type
activities are very important in language learning and very easy
to invent.

Note

In some of the activities the class will be working with
measurements of various kinds, including sizes, speeds, and
weights. Unless you and all your students share a common
system, you will need to establish a standard before you begin
the activity. A conversion chart might be useful.

3.1 Numbers: my numbers

LEVEL

1–3; adults

TIME

30 minutes

LANGUAGE

How to say age, weight, height, measurements, and sizes,
telephone number, house number, date of birth

PROCEDURE

1 Ask each student to rule a left-hand margin and then draw a
line down the middle of a sheet of paper. Demonstrate this on
the board. On the left-hand side of the centre line write, 'My
real . . .' and on the right-hand side, 'My ideal . . .'. Write 'Age'
in the left-hand margin. Ask the students to do the same on their
sheets of paper.

2 Tell the students your real age (mine's 47) and your ideal age
(mine's 20). Explain that they must decide whether to write their
real or their ideal age (or both) in the appropriate column(s). So,
if I wrote both, my paper would look like this:

	My real	My ideal
Age	47	20

3 Continue writing up left-hand margin entries for the students to copy before writing in their own real or ideal entries. Good categories include weight, height, waist measurement, dress/suit size, shoe size. You can also dictate less personal categories like birthday, house number, post code, and telephone number. All the time complete your own profile on the board.

4 Once the profiles are complete, go through yours turning the numbers into spoken words. For example, 'I'm forty-seven', 'My ideal age is twenty', etc. Pause after each sentence to allow any member of the class who wants to to turn their numbers into a spoken sentence.

5 Ask the students to work in pairs, telling each other about themselves and calling you over whenever they need help.

3.2 Numbers: my inventory

LEVEL   1–4; children and adults

TIME   15 minutes upwards

MATERIALS   A bilingual dictionary for every two students

LANGUAGE   I own [number] [name of article]; plural forms

PROCEDURE   1 Tell each student to write 'I own . . .' on a sheet of paper and then think of things they own. Each time they think of something, they should think how many of the articles they own. For example, for 'book', perhaps '500'. Each student should make a list of articles they own, together with the number of each article. Encourage the use of dictionaries.

2 Ask students to compare their lists and then display them on the wall.

VARIATION 1   This activity also works well when you specify the room students should think of or the area (for example, clothes, sports equipment, etc.).

VARIATION 2   In classes where it would be tactless or would make problems to list possessions, tell each student at Step 1 to write 'I would like to own . . .'.

COMMENTS   You can return to this activity again and again. As well as being a very good way of building up vocabulary in areas where students want to learn English words, it provides incidental practice with numbers and plurals.

3.3 Numbers: writing by numbers

LEVEL   2–4; children and adults

TIME   15 minutes

LANGUAGE   Numbers as they are used

PREPARATION   Make a list of cardinal numbers, dates (day, month, year), telephone numbers, train times, sums of money, etc.

PROCEDURE   Dictate this list to the students using only numbers—for example, if one of the items on your list was £4.99, you would simply say, 'Four ninety-nine'. As you dictate, the students write down, either in English or in their mother tongue, the type of number they think they are hearing—for example, 'Sum of money' or 'price'.

VARIATION	A good variation is to do this with speeds—the students have to write down the animal or machine which travels at the speeds you read out. Before you do this, remember to check whether your students are more familiar with miles or kilometres.
COMMENTS	Students are always interested in acquiring this knowledge as using it outside the classroom gives them a strong sense of achievement. They particularly like to know all the different ways of saying the number '0' in the various contexts in which it occurs. And you can have a bit of fun by adding one or two unguessables at the end, like 'thirteen-seventy-two' (the size of your car engine) and 'six' (the time the last post goes in your street)—note that there is important new language to be learnt from these fun examples too.

3.4 Numbers: lucky numbers

LEVEL	2–4; children and adults
TIME	30 minutes
LANGUAGE	Numbers; 'what', 'why', and 'because' sentences
PROCEDURE	1 Ask each student to make a list of all their classmates.

2 Each student should think of a number that has been lucky for them.

3 Ask the students to circulate, getting information from each other about their lucky numbers. Provide them with model sentences like the following:

What is your lucky number?
Why is [number] lucky for you?
Because . . .

Each student should write down the lucky numbers and the reason why they are lucky for as many members of the class as is possible in the time.

VARIATION	There are several possible alternatives to lucky numbers, including important dates, favourite colours, significant mother-tongue words, etc.

3.5 Numbers: number biographies

LEVEL 3–4; adults

TIME 40 minutes

LANGUAGE Reading numbers aloud, particularly years

PROCEDURE 1 Write the following on the board: house number, car number, telephone number, immediate family.

2 Ask each student to construct a number biography by choosing one or more of the categories on the board and writing down

– all the house numbers and roads they have lived at, with dates
– all the car numbers and makes of cars they or their family have owned, with dates
– all the telephone numbers they have ever had, with dates
– the number of living members of their immediate family, with dates of birth. (Explain that they should include grandparents, uncles and aunts, parents, children, nephews and nieces, grandchildren.)

3 Do the same thing yourself on the board. For example, if I chose house numbers and roads, I might write down

1946–1948   8 Firs Grove
1948–1964 30 Hollin Lane
1964–1968 46 Hollin Lane
etc.

Allow 20 minutes.

4 With small groups, ask each student to relate their biography to their classmates. With larger classes, ask the students to do this in groups of four or five. Before they start this phase, provide a model by relating your own biography. For example, 'From 1946 to 1948, my parents and I lived at 8 Firs Grove,' etc.

COMMENTS Writing the biography is easy in the sense that the students will be thinking in their mother tongue(s). Talking it through in English will be much more difficult. You will need to provide a model for each number category in Step 2.

3.6 Telling the time: the classroom as clock

LEVEL

3–4; children

TIME

Day 1, 30 minutes; day 2, 30 minutes; day 3, 30 minutes

MATERIALS

You need a classroom where it is possible to arrange the chairs in a circle

LANGUAGE

The language used to tell the time

PREPARATION

Arrange twelve chairs in a circle, preferably in the middle of the classroom. They should be numbered from 1 to 12.

PROCEDURE

Day 1: Demonstrating how to tell the time

1 Ask for two volunteers. Sit one volunteer in the chair marked 12. Ask the second volunteer to stand behind the chair marked 1. Then say, 'It's one o'clock'. Ask the volunteer to move to chair 2. Say, 'It's two o'clock'. Continue round the clockface encouraging the students to say the time with you.

2 Ask the first volunteer to sit in the chair marked 6, and with the second volunteer standing behind the chair marked 1, say, 'It's half past one'. Continue moving the second volunteer round the clockface, saying the time as you do.

3 Repeat Step 2 with the first volunteer sitting in the chair marked 3 ('It's quarter past . . .'), and then with the volunteer sitting in the chair marked 9 ('It's quarter to . . .').

Day 2: Demonstrating how to tell the time

Ask for two more volunteers and repeat the previous day's routine, this time concentrating on the other times, i.e. 'It's five past . . .', 'It's ten past . . .', 'It's twenty past . . .', 'It's twenty-five past . . .', 'It's twenty-five to . . .', etc.

Day 3: Practice

1 Sit a student in each of the twelve chairs and ask for two volunteers. Instruct one volunteer to run clockwise round the outside of the circle and the other to run anti-clockwise round the inside of the circle. Explain that the outer runner represents minutes and the inner runner represents hours, and that when you shout 'Time' the runners will stop and the students will tell the time.

2 After four or five goes, ask for two new volunteers and continue the game.

COMMENTS

You can only do this activity with children (and adults) who know how to tell the time.

Acknowledgement
This idea was thought out by Anna Korea.

3.7 Telling the time: talking about the time

LEVEL   2–3; children and adults

TIME   20–30 minutes

LANGUAGE   At [number] o'clock I feel [adjective]

PREPARATION   Draw a large clockface on the board or on a sheet of A3 paper but without the numbers 6 and 7 (since most people's day runs from 8.00 a.m. to 5.00 p.m.).

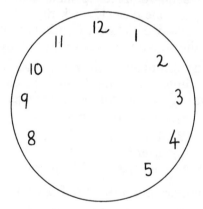

PROCEDURE   1 Ask each learner to copy the clockface into their exercise book, or if you prefer to make a wall display, on to a sheet of paper.

2 Brainstorm a list of the adjectives the class already know, such as happy, hungry, tired, sleepy, excited, etc. You may also want to add one or two new words. (If you are keeping a list of adjectives displayed on the wall, work with this list.)

3 Provide the class with the following frame:

At _____ o'clock I feel _____.

and ask each student to complete the frame so as to make a sentence which is true for them. For example:

At two o'clock I feel lazy.

They should write their sentences down.

4 You have a number of options at this stage:

- Ask the student with the earliest time to say their sentence first; each student then follows with theirs to make a class day from early in the morning to late afternoon.
- Ask the students to arrange themselves in a circle by time; in a circle from most to least positive; so as to make a logical progression (for example, happy—hungry—sleepy).
- Ask the students to circulate telling each other their sentences. When they return to their places, how many of their classmates' sentences can they recall?
- Ask the students to find a classmate who feels different from them at the same time of the day.
- Ask each student to write a four-line 'poem', with each line containing a different statement about their feelings at different times of the day.

VARIATION 1

You can do the same activity with evening and night hours. This time leave out the numbers 3, 4, and 5. You will need to specify times as follows:

At _____ o'clock in the evening I feel _____ (for 6 and 7 o'clock).

At _____ o'clock at night I feel _____ (for 8, 9, 10, and 11 o'clock).

At midnight I feel _____.

At _____ o'clock in the morning I feel _____ (for 1 and 2 o'clock).

VARIATION 2

This activity can also be used for practising other structures such as 'I like . . .ing at . . .', 'I [action verb] at . . .'.

VARIATION 3

The students can construct a day in the life of a class member, or any other person, using this structure.

Acknowledgements

Melanie Ellis suggested finding classmates with the same time and different feelings and John Morgan suggested Variation 3.

3.8 Days of the week: weekday collage

LEVEL	1–4; adults and children
TIME	30 minutes
MATERIALS	Colour magazines, scissors, glue, large sheets of paper
LANGUAGE	Names of days of the week

PROCEDURE

1 Write the names of the days of the week on the board.

2 Divide the class into seven groups and distribute colour magazines. Ask each group to find pictures of people which they can associate with each day of the week. Allow ten minutes.

3 Allocate one weekday to each group and ask all the groups to give their pictures for that weekday to the appropriate group.

4 Each group now makes a collage for their weekday and displays this on the wall.

COMMENTS

1 Although the only language specified for this activity is the names of the days of the week, the students are obliged to discuss the appropriacy of each picture in relation to their chosen day. In practice, this means that quite a lot of language is required to do the job really well, although the task can be done even by level 1 beginners.

2 The English name for each weekday is thus associated with the feelings that the day inspires.

3.9 Months: in January I feel . . .

LEVEL	1–4; adults and children; smaller classes are best because large classes require too many materials
TIME	30 minutes
MATERIALS	Large sheets of paper, colour magazines, scissors, glue
LANGUAGE	In [month] I feel [happy/sad/cold/excited] and I [go to the seaside/go skiing/stay indoors/watch television]

PREPARATION   Prepare one large sheet of paper (for example, A3) for each
student, with 'In' plus the name of a month in the top left-hand
corner. You will need at least twelve sheets so that each month is
represented. Near the bottom of each sheet, write 'I feel' in a
balloon with plenty of space, and 'and I' in a similar balloon next
to it:

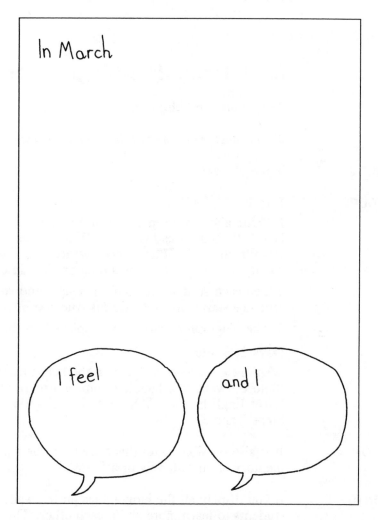

There should be one sheet for each student; in classes of fewer
than twelve students, there should be a sheet for each month.

PROCEDURE   1 Ask each student to choose a sheet for a month that they have
feelings about. Make colour magazines, scissors, and glue
available.

2 Each student looks for pictures that are relevant to their
chosen month, cuts them out, and assembles them collage-style
on their month sheet.

3 Each student then writes in the first balloon how they feel in the month in question and in the second what they do.

4 The completed sheets make a nice wall display.

VARIATION

You can pair students for this activity: substitute 'we' for 'I' in the balloons.

3.10 Time: time biographies

LEVEL

3–4; adults and children

TIME

25–30 minutes a day for three or four days

LANGUAGE

Time clauses

PROCEDURE

Day 1

1 Write about ten sentence starters like the following on the board: 'When I was five . . .', 'When I was ten . . .', 'When I was fifteen . . .', 'When I was twenty . . .', 'When I was twenty-five . . .', etc. (depending on the age of your students).

2 Tell each student to choose five ages and complete each sentence starter in a way that is true and interesting.

3 The biographies should be displayed on the wall.

Days 2, 3, etc.

Write new sentence starters on the board using formulas such as: 'Before I went to school/left home/got married/broke a bone/ learnt English . . .', 'Whenever I . . .', 'While I . . .', and repeat Steps 2 and 3.

VARIATION

It is also possible to do this activity in the name of another member of one's family or a friend.

COMMENTS

If you display all the biographies on the wall, this allows the students to learn more about each other. The display can be used as the basis of several other activities, including talking to each other about their biographies, comparing members of the class at the same time or in the same situation, and producing graphs and other quantified summaries.

3.11 Colours: colour dictation

LEVEL	2–4; adults and children
TIME	10 minutes
MATERIALS	Coloured pens or pencils for Variations 2 and 3
LANGUAGE	Vocabulary items and associated colour terms
PREPARATION	Make a list of words which could be associated with colours. Good examples include: stop, go, love, sky, moon.
PROCEDURE	1 Ensure that the students know the names of the colours. Illustrate where necessary with coloured objects.
	2 Dictate the prepared list. Instead of writing the words they hear, the students should write down the colour they associate with the word. You may mime words and the students may use dictionaries.
VARIATION 1	Dictate colour words. Allow a minute between words while the students write down all the objects in the classroom of that colour. Allow the use of dictionaries.
VARIATION 2	Prepare a short dictation in which every sentence contains a colour word. When you dictate, the students use a pen of the appropriate colour for each sentence.
VARIATION 3	Ask the students to copy any of the lists of vocabulary displayed in the classroom, but to use a pen of whatever colour they feel is appropriate for each item. The results can be displayed on the wall and compared.

3.12 Colours: all about me

LEVEL	2–4; adults and children
TIME	25 minutes
MATERIALS	Coloured pens or pencils for Variation 1
LANGUAGE	My [hair/shirt etc.] is [colour word]
PROCEDURE	1 Write a list of words on the board which describe either physical features or articles of clothing (for example, eyes, skin, shoes, shirt).

2 Tell each student to write sentences using the format, 'My [word from board] is [colour word]'. Let the students help each other and use dictionaries.

VARIATION 1

With children (and even sometimes with adults), encourage them to draw themselves as they have described themselves and display the finished work on the wall.

VARIATION 2

Another way of doing this activity is to ask students to name the colour of their best shoes/sweater, etc.

3.13 Colours: rainbow people

LEVEL

1–3; children

TIME

30 minutes approx. (depending on class size)

MATERIALS

Pictures of well-known people (see Preparation); a set of coloured pens, paints, or chalks for the teacher; and one set of coloured pens or pencils for every five to six students

LANGUAGE

Colour words

PREPARATION

Ask each student to bring to class a newspaper or magazine picture of someone famous who they like. The pictures should be cut out and mounted on a sheet of paper.

PROCEDURE

1 Pre-teach the names of the colours. This is much easier if you have coloured chalk, coloured pens, or a paintbox.

2 Explain that everyone will take a turn at displaying their picture. When this happens, each student will say the colour they associate with the person in the picture.

3 Ask the first student to show their picture and each member of the class to name the colour they associate with it. The student writes down all the colours suggested and records how often each colour is mentioned.

4 When all the pictures have been shown, allow time for the students to construct colour rainbows around their pictures. The rainbow must be an accurate reflection of how often each colour was mentioned for each picture.

5 The class makes a wall display of the 'Rainbow People', using their aesthetic judgement to arrange them in an appropriate order.

3.14 Colours: colour bingo

LEVEL   2–4; children

TIME   30 minutes to make bingo cards + 10 minutes per game

MATERIALS   One card divided into 12 segments, 12 small pieces of paper, and a set of coloured pens, pencils, or paints for each student; an empty box

LANGUAGE   Understanding simple questions; names of colours

PREPARATION   1 Prepare one card divided into 12 segments and 12 small pieces of paper for each student.

2 Prepare 12 simple questions to which the answer will be the name of a colour. Possible questions include: 'What's your favourite colour?', 'What's your least favourite colour?', 'What colour is your hair?'

PROCEDURE   1 Distribute the cards and the small pieces of paper.

2 Ask the first question, and allow the students time to colour or paint their answer into the first segment on the card. Each student also colours or paints one of the small pieces of paper and puts it into the empty box.

3 Continue with the other 11 questions until all the segments and small pieces of paper are coloured in. Most students will have more than one segment in the same colour—this does not matter.

4 Invite a student to take a coloured piece of paper out of the box and call out the colour. Anyone who has one or more segments in this colour on their card should mark them with a small tick.

5 Choose further students to repeat Step 4. As soon as someone has ticked all their segments, they shout 'Bingo!' to win the game.

COMMENTS   1 This activity begins with each student silently using a colour to show they have understood a question. In the 'Bingo' phase, the students practise both production and comprehension.

2 You may decide to complete a card too or demonstrate what to do on a board divided into 12 segments.

Acknowledgement

This is Anna Korea's idea.

3.15 Summing it all up

LEVEL

3–4; children and adults

TIME

30 minutes

LANGUAGE

I can count to 100, I can spell my name, I can tell the time

PROCEDURE

1 Ask each student to take a large sheet of paper and spend 15 minutes listing all the things they can do in English. Each sentence should begin with the words 'I can . . .'.

2 After 15 minutes, ask each student to write one more achievement, this time one that had not occurred to them and which they do not expect anyone else to have thought of. For example, 'I can do a card trick in English'. (Allow the use of dictionaries if necessary at this point.)

3 Ask the students to compare achievements orally for five minutes.

4 Allow five more minutes for each student to add to their own list in the light of achievements claimed by classmates.

5 As a further option, you can ask some students to demonstrate their claims too.

COMMENTS

1 It is a good idea to repeat this activity at fortnightly intervals. You can also encourage students to keep achievement diaries (see 10.5, 'Diary ideas').

2 It adds to class morale to display these achievements on the wall. The teacher can also complete one for the average class member. This is useful because it allows the students to compare what they think they can do with what the teacher thinks they have been taught to do.

4 Language basics

This chapter contains eleven activities which introduce several of the basic syntactic structures and phonological features of English. The structural activities are found in the first part of the chapter and the phonological ones in the second part.

In the case of English phonology, it is important to know that the phonetic realization of a segment is conditioned by the environment in which it occurs. Thus the first vowel of 'photograph' is pronounced differently from the first vowel of 'photographer'. Activity 4.8 is based on this feature of English. Similarly, the assignment of sentence stress depends on the nature of the sentence itself rather than on the quality of any particular segment within it. Activities 4.9 and 4.11 are based on this feature of English. These suprasegmental elements of phonology are not usually so salient to learners as the segmental, but are certainly more important in intelligible communication. It is for this reason that four of the five phonology activities focus on suprasegmental features. Most of these activities are more difficult than those in the previous chapter.

4.1 The grand tour

LEVEL

2–4; adults and children

TIME

20 minutes

LANGUAGE

Prepositions and present progressive form: **We are [verb]ing along/through/past/at/into [noun]**

PROCEDURE

1 Ask the class to stand up and follow you.

2 Walk through the classroom door into the corridor and say, 'I am walking through the door'. As the students follow you, indicate that they should either repeat individually what you have said or say collectively, 'We are walking through the door', depending on what you decide is best for them.

3 Continue your tour of the school, describing your progress with sentences containing appropriate prepositions. For example, 'I am walking along the corridor', 'I am walking past the staffroom', 'I am looking at the notice board', 'I am going into the library'.

VARIATION 1	Before you start this tour, you can describe what you are *going to* do, and when you come back the class can tell you what they *did*.
VARIATION 2	You can allow members of the class to take responsibility for devising the route and the actions taken.
VARIATION 3	If you wish, you can also introduce a wide range of verbs such as 'creep' and 'hop' into your tour.
COMMENTS	This activity has a TPR dimension and works in much the same way—the students learn more effectively through associating movement and language.

Acknowledgement

This is Geri Smyth's idea. She teaches at Jordanhill College of Education.

4.2 Exotic experiences

LEVEL	**3–4; adults and children**
TIME	**30 minutes**
LANGUAGE	**Present perfect form: 'I've . . .'**
PROCEDURE	1 Tell the students about three striking experiences you have had using the formula 'I've . . .'. For example, 'I've been to China, I've seen the Pope, and I've climbed Mount Fuji.' 2 Ask each student to write down three striking experiences they have had using the same formula. Provide assistance where necessary. 3 Choose a student and ask them the following question: '[Name], what have you done?' The student replies, 'I've x, I've y, and I've z.' You can encourage the class to make loud 'ooh-aah' noises at this stage, if you wish. 4 The student who had related their experiences now asks another student what they have done, and Step 3 is repeated.
COMMENTS	It could be argued that the present perfect should only be taught in sentences where there is present continuation such as, 'I've just bought a computer and now I'm learning to use it'. But these structures are beyond beginner level. This activity brings home to students how past events live in their minds and are part of their present.

4.3 In the bag

LEVEL   3–4; adults and children

TIME   30 minutes

LANGUAGE   Questions with 'have got'; lists of vocabulary items; questions like 'What has [name] got in his/her [pocket]?'

PROCEDURE   1 Ask each student to take a sheet of paper and make a list of one of the following:
– everything they have in their pockets
– everything they have in their handbag or wallet
– everything they keep in their bathroom
– everything they keep in the wardrobe in their bedroom
– everything they keep in the largest drawer in their kitchen
– everything they keep in their fridge.

Allow the use of dictionaries.

2 Tell the students to display their lists on their desks, then to circulate reading their classmates' lists and trying to memorize them.

3 Tell the students to return to their desks. Each student should ask the class a question about one of their classmates whose topic (pocket, handbag, etc.) they remember. They should use the form 'What has [name] got in his/her [pocket/handbag]?' The other students try to answer.

4.4 Sentence starters

LEVEL   3–4; children and adults

TIME   10 minutes in class + homework + 30 minutes in class

LANGUAGE   Topic + comment structure; sentence starters such as, 'This weekend . . .' and 'Our class . . .' + continuations

PROCEDURE   Lesson 1

1 Write two sentence starters such as 'This weekend . . .' and 'Our class . . .' on the board. Ask for suggested ways of completing them and write these on the board.

2 Ask each student to think of two original sentence starters of their own for homework, write each at the top of a separate piece of paper, underline it, and complete each sentence in a way that is true for them. They should bring their sentences to class for the next lesson.

Lesson 2

1 Ask each student to read out their sentence starters (but not complete sentences). The other students write down all the starters.

2 Either ask the students to blu-tack their two homework sheets to the wall, or, where this is not possible, display them on their desks.

3 Allow 20 minutes for each student to complete as many of the starters with their own original completions as possible. Each new sentence should be added to the sheet with that sentence starter at the top.

COMMENTS

1 Separating making sentences into these two phases (starter plus completion) is a very enabling activity because most students can think of starters readily enough even if they have to get to English via their mother tongues.

2 Choosing which starters to complete (Step 3) is fun, allows students to choose the language that meets their individual needs, and enables them to say something about themselves.

4.5 Interviewing a celebrity

LEVEL

3–4; adults and children

TIME

35 minutes

LANGUAGE

Making questions: What is the [superlative + noun] you've ever [verb]?

PROCEDURE

1 Ask each member of the class the question, 'What is the best film you've ever seen?'

2 Explain that each member of the class should think up a question in this form but about a topic other than films. This will mean substituting another superlative for the word 'best', a new noun for the word 'film', and an appropriate verb for the word 'seen'—for example, 'What's the funniest book you've ever read?'

3 When everyone has invented a question, ask for a volunteer to come and sit in front of the class and answer all the questions.

VARIATION If you wish, ask the volunteer to answer the questions as though they were a well-known politician, entertainer, sports personality, etc.

COMMENTS This introduces superlatives naturally and without contrasting them with comparatives.

4.6 Good and bad pairs

LEVEL 1–2; children and adults

TIME 20 minutes

MATERIALS Lots of magazine pictures, address labels (optional)

LANGUAGE The names of the letters of the alphabet

PREPARATION Choose lots of magazine pictures in a single category such as people (they needn't be well-known people), food and drink, articles of clothing, etc. Label each picture with a different letter of the alphabet. It is important that these are big enough to be seen, so it is a good idea to write them on address labels and stick the address label to the picture. You also need to decide whether to use upper or lower case (or both). Display the prepared pictures on one wall—do not arrange them alphabetically.

PROCEDURE 1 Call out pairs of letters. The students say 'Yes' if they think two pictures go well together and 'No' if they do not.

2 Ask the students to take turns at calling out pairs of letters.

VARIATION 1 If you do this activity twice (i.e. with two different categories of picture), leave the first set of pictures on the walls and then next time combine them with the second set. People and food go well together, for example.

VARIATION 2 If your pictures are of different objects (for example, different kinds of food), spell the object shown in one of the pictures and ask the students to call out the letter of the picture as soon as they recognize what you are spelling.

Acknowledgement

Gerry Kenny's ideas for alphabet learning inspired this activity.

4.7 Sound bingo

LEVEL	3–4; children and adults
TIME	50 minutes (25 if you make Step 2 a homework activity)
MATERIALS	Bingo cards (see Preparation)
LANGUAGE	Distinctive phonoligcal features such as [+voice] as in 'ridge' (/ridʒ/) and [−voice] as in 'rich' (/ritʃ/)
PREPARATION	Prepare a blank bingo card with 15 squares for each student.

PROCEDURE

1 Write the following words on the board:

late	pin	walk	feet	seed	dock	bet	fit
bin	ball	least	write	dish	bit	peas	rich
seat	cot	fail	rate	got	paul	ditch	cut
lug	rug	dug	weep	feed	peace	ride	work
light	beat	bed	list	duck	sit	ridge	vale

2 Tell the students to copy them down and look up their meanings in their dictionaries. Give help where necessary. Or ask the students to look their meanings up for homework and continue with Step 3 the following day.

3 Each student should choose 15 words to write on their bingo cards.

4 Dictate the words one by one in random order. As you dictate, number each word. For example:

1 ridge
2 fail

and so on.

Make a list yourself. When the students think they hear a word that appears on their card, they should write the number in the square that the word appears in.

5 As soon as a student thinks they have completed their card, they shout 'Bingo!'.

6 When someone shouts 'Bingo!', ask the students to form pairs so they can compare their work. Call out the words again slowly one by one, writing any problematical ones on the board.

VARIATION

After Step 1, ask the students to look up 15 of the words in their dictionaries and write the mother-tongue equivalents in the squares on their bingo cards. When you call the words in English, the students write the number of the word in the square in which the appropriate translation appears. If you use translation, bingo does not need to be phonetic. You can use it to teach new vocabulary, for example.

COMMENTS

Most students find this discrete listening activity very difficult indeed and make lots of mistakes. If you number each word you call out at Step 4, this makes it much easier later when the students check whether they really did hear what they thought they heard. It also enables you to see which pairs of words were problematical and to demonstrate the differences.

4.8 Polysyllabic stress

LEVEL

3–4; adults

TIME

5–10 minutes whenever you encounter a polysyllabic word

MATERIALS

Wall chart (see Preparation)

LANGUAGE

Word stress on polysyllabic words

PREPARATION

Make a wall chart with five columns in such a way that the third column is highlighted—perhaps in a different colour or with thicker lines. For example:

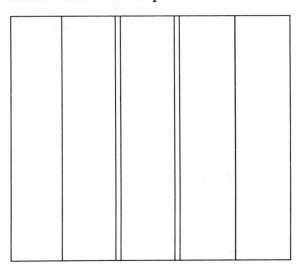

PROCEDURE

1 Whenever you come across a polysyllabic word in class, write it on the wall chart in such a way that the stressed syllable is in the highlighted column. Ask the students for guidance before you write. If you come across a word which can be lengthened or shortened as a result of the presence/absence of derivational morphology, write both/all of the versions up at the same time. In this way, the students will see that the main stress in 'photograph' and 'photographer' does not fall on the same syllable.

		pho	to	graph
	pho	to	graph	er

2 Each time you write a word on the board, give time for everyone to practise saying it—and any other words already written up which they want to practise.

VARIATION

VARIATION

When this idea is well established, you may want to make sure that the students understand the principle of reduced vowels. This can be done by writing all schwa vowels in a particular colour such as red. Thus, the second vowel of 'photograph' and the first, third, and fourth vowels of 'photographer' would be written in red.

COMMENTS

This activity also helps the students to become aware that the writing system of English is an unreliable guide to pronunciation.

4.9 Talk and stress

LEVEL

2–4; adults

TIME

25 minutes

LANGUAGE

Sentence stress

PROCEDURE

1 Ask each student to write five sentences about themselves. The first should be, 'My name's . . .' and each of the others should contain either one or two more words and/or one or two different words from the previous one.

2 When everyone has written their sentences, write yours on the board. Good examples are:

My name's [Peter].
My first name's [Peter].
My name's [Peter Grundy].
I think my name's [Peter Grundy].
I think your name's [Ahmad].

Explain that each sentence has two principal stresses. Demonstrate how your sentences should be stressed:

<u>My</u> name's <u>Peter</u>.
My <u>first</u> name's <u>Peter</u>.
<u>My</u> name's Peter <u>Grundy</u>.
I <u>think</u> my name's <u>Peter</u> <u>Grundy</u>.
I think <u>your</u> name's <u>Ahmad</u>.

3 Ask each student to spend two or three minutes trying to place the stresses in their sentences.

4 Ask for a volunteer to declare their sentences with the appropriate stresses. If the student misplaces a stress, provide a correct model. Continue until the class tires of the activity.

VARIATION 1

If you have problems giving the instructions at Step 1, you can use your own sentences as a model.

VARIATION 2

Once the class understands the idea, you can repeat it often. It works well when you have a theme such as 'what I do in the morning' or 'how I spent Sunday'. This makes the sentences worth listening to for their content as well.

COMMENTS

The students probably learn more from listening to each other and rehearsing their own sentences in their heads than from trying to declare them, so you do not need to be concerned if not every member of the class wants or gets a turn.

4.10 Hearing word boundaries

LEVEL

3–4; adults and children

TIME

20 minutes

MATERIALS

Text (see Preparation)

LANGUAGE

Recognizing words and word boundaries

PREPARATION Choose a text which is quite a lot harder than your students can understand. Poems are best. Make a photocopy.

PROCEDURE **1** If your students are willing to work with their eyes shut, ask them to relax and close their eyes. Explain that you will read a poem to them and that you just want them to listen out for any words that they can identify.

2 Read the text two or three times while the students listen.

3 Ask the students to write down any words they identified, if possible in the order in which they occurred in the text.

4 Ask the students to compare their results with a neighbour.

5 Read the text for the last time and allow a few more minutes for adding any further words to the list.

6 Display the text on the wall and tell the students that they should study it at the end of the lesson.

VARIATION **1** Choose a text with fewer words than there are chairs in your classroom. Follow Steps 1 and 2 above.

2 Number the chairs from 1 to however how many there are in the classroom.

3 Then ask the students to choose one of the words they heard and go and sit in the chair which they think corresponds to the place in the poem where their word occurs. So, if a student thinks their word is the twentieth in the poem, they sit in chair number 20. Then read the poem word by word, indicating which chair each word goes with, and allowing time for each student to move to the appropriate chair.

COMMENTS **1** This activity also works well with short newspaper articles, particularly topical stories.

2 Although it may seem a deceptively simple activity, this actually provides practice in the vital skill of recognizing word boundaries. When we hear a foreign language which we do not know, the most difficult problem is identifying word boundaries. Once we can do this, we can usually get the gist and begin to experience the satisfaction of being a successful second language learner.

4.11 Fregzampl

LEVEL **3–4; adults**

TIME **15 minutes**

MATERIALS **Prepared texts**

LANGUAGE **Suprasegmental phonology—sentence stress and pronunciation**

PREPARATION

This activity takes quite a lot of preparation.

1 Choose a short passage, such as a dialogue from your coursebook or the beginning of a story you are going to tell or read.

2 Write a version of it in which each sense unit is typed, enlarged, and presented on a separate card. Each sense unit should be written as a single continuous text without word boundaries. Use a 'natural' spelling system and underline the two main stresses in each unit. Thus, the opening of the children's story *Mr Noisy* would look like this:

MrNoisywzuveryverynoisypersonindeed
fregzampl
ifMrNoisywzreadingthistorytyou
he'dbishoutingutthtopv(h)izvoice
ndthtopvMrNoisy'svoice
iz
averyloudplaceindeed
youcnhearituhundredmilesaway
fregzampl
w(h)enmos(t)peoplesneeze
youcnhearthminthnex(t)room
buthuhuhuhutshoo
w(h)enMrNoisysneezesyoucnhear(h)iminthnex(t)country

PROCEDURE

1 After you have read and worked on the dialogue or text as it appears in the coursebook, ask the students to close their books. Hold up the first card-mounted sense unit and say it as a continuous structure, making the sentence stresses prominent. Continue with the second, and so on until the end of the prepared text.

2 Repeat the process, this time with the students accompanying you chorally.

3 Keep on practising until the students feel confident enough to read the text individually as a native speaker would.

COMMENTS

This is a very valuable activity, although it is quite troublesome to prepare. It shows the students that word boundaries are not really detectable in continuous speech, it gives practice in marking stress, and because the text is not easily readable, it frees the students from close, phonic reliance on a script when they read.

5 Roman script

When we hear someone talk in an informed way or read something written by someone who has thought more carefully about the topic than us, we are suddenly, and often painfully, aware of the extent of our own ignorance. I had one of these eye-opening experiences some years ago when I read Ian White's MA dissertation 'Ethnocentric, Graphological and Linguistic Assumptions in English Language Teaching'. Since then, I have been unable to put out of my mind the real difficulties that learners without Roman script have, and how little we seem to take this on board in the preparation of materials.

Ian White reflects with real care on his experiences working with early stage learners without Roman script in Saudi Arabia. He points out that virtually all beginners' coursebooks assume that the students can recognize individual letters and groups of letters in upper and lower case, in printed and handwritten forms, even when presented in a variety of fonts and print sizes whose functions must be far from clear.

He goes on to describe how, in the productive mode, students experience real difficulties with ascenders and descenders, letter spacing, achieving consistent script slant, maintaining a line, with upper and lower case, and with punctuation placement. He claims—surely correctly—that we largely ignore the problem of both the receptive and productive mastery of script and assume that it will sort itself out with time. He suggests that this may be partly a function of our having mastered the Roman script so successfully ourselves that we forget the immense nature of our achievement and somehow imagine that it is second nature to our learners just as it is to ourselves. And to reinforce this point, he observes that there had only been three articles on handwriting in the *ELT Journal* in the forty-two years of its existence up to the time of his writing. (Six more years have now passed, and the tally of handwriting articles remains at three.)

Following Ball (1986), White points out that difficulties with Roman script lead to many other problems, including reading difficulties, failure to keep pace with other students in the writing phases of lessons, inability to take notes effectively in academic classes, and heightened tension causing further errors in spelling and structure. At this point, White observes that the use of print script compounds handwriting problems, since it is particularly slow and causes students to focus on discrete segments. It is also perceived as infantile. He therefore goes on to argue that cursive is to be preferred to print script for adult learners.

Ian White's observations have lived with me since I first read his dissertation. The relatively large number of script activities in this chapter reflect the influence of his arguments.

There are a number of other points that should be borne in mind when teaching Roman script:

1 The print styles and fonts students encounter will inevitably be very varied. As an illustration, several different initial-position instances of the letter 't' from British national daily newspaper mastheads are given below:

2 There is a reasonable range of handwriting practice books available. Try to integrate these into your work rather than leave them entirely to self-study sessions. Calligraphy competitions in which the teacher takes part are good fun (particularly when entries are under pseudonyms).

3 Remember that as well as the difficulties of forming characters, when they are representing speech in writing, your students will first have to decide which characters to choose. When they hear the phoneme [k] for example, they must decide if it is to be realized as 'c' (cat), 'k' (trek), 'kk' (trekking), 'ck' (sick), 'ch' (school), 'Ch' (Christmas), 'q' or arguably 'qu' (queen), 'que' (Basque), 'cc' (occur), 'kh' (khaki), 'x' (extra), or 'cu' (biscuit). And [k] is by no means the most problematical phoneme from this point of view.

4 Mastering Roman script is not strictly a language learning activity at all, merely an extra burden for some beginners.

5 Expect different problems for learners with different script systems such as right-left cursive (Arabic), ideographic non-alphabetic (Chinese), partially overlapping with Roman (Cyrillic), heavy reliance on diacritics, etc.

6 At the level of comprehension, your students will typically be trying to learn how to recognize words, whereas at the level of production they will be concentrating on characters. For example, most people who find themselves in countries where they cannot read the script quickly learn how 'Ladies' and 'Gentlemen' are represented. This means that your students will be mastering script in two different ways depending on the skill they are exercising.

7 It is worth remembering that in virtually every country in the world students will have seen several words written in Roman script, even if their own script is non-Roman. Words like 'Taxi' and 'Hotel' are very common (although 'Hotel' is also frequently written vertically). (See 5.11, 'Recognizing familiar words'.)

8 Learners may be able, or even keen, to work on spoken language for some while before learning Roman script. They may want to learn the script in a way that integrates it with language learning or they may want to treat it as relatively separate. There are arguments for both approaches of course—what matters is that you have taken a conscious decision.

9 How phonic will you make your sessions on script? The more phonic you make them, the more counter-intuitive the script will seem. Because sound–spelling correspondences in English are variable, a whole-word approach not only to the recognition but even to the production of script can seem more logical than a strictly alphabetic, segmental one.

Finally, imagine the difficulties you might face learning to read (recognize) and write (produce) a script with which you were unfamiliar. Try to approach the activities in this chapter from that perspective. They focus on copying (activities 5.1 to 5.5), evaluating (activities 5.6 to 5.8), matching (5.9), and recognition (activities 5.10 and 5.11).

5.1 Upper and lower case

LEVEL   1–2; adults and children

TIME   30 minutes

LANGUAGE   Familiarization with upper- and lower-case characters

PROCEDURE   1 Ask each student to write their name in English, and after their name to write or copy out the English alphabet in lower case until they get to the first letter of their name, which they should write in upper case. So a student called Maria will write:

a b c d e f g h i j k l M

2 The students now continue until they reach the second letter of their name, and so on until their name is highlighted in upper case in a continuous lower-case alphabet:

a b c d e f g h i j k l M n o p q r s t u v w x y z A b c d e f g h
i j k l m n o p q R s t u v w x y z a b c d e f g h I j k l m n o p
q r s t u v w x y z A

Encourage artistic variations which help the students to practise spacing, for example:

a b c d e f g h i j k l M
n o p q r s t u v w x y z A
b c d e f g h i j k l m n o p q R
s t u v w x y z a b c d e f g h I
j k l m n o p q r s t u v w x y z A

3 Repeat this with a number of other categories such as home town, occupation (for adults), names of other family members, etc. These activities result in individual pieces of work which make interesting wall displays. If they are anonymous, fellow students can try to identify the authors.

VARIATION 1

Lots of variations on this theme are possible, including simpler activities such as writing lists of all those present in upper case and any absentees in lower case.

VARIATION 2

Another possibility is to dictate (or let the students dictate) the names of entertainers, sports figures, or politicians, which members of the class can write down in upper case if they like them and lower case if they do not.

VARIATION 3

Yet another possibility is to use upper and lower case in the alphabet as a basis for displaying the composition of sports teams, characters in plays, etc. For example, the nationality composition of my class might look like this:

a
BRAZILIAN
CHINESE, CZECH
d
e
f
GERMAN
HUNGARIAN
IRANIAN, ITALIAN
JAPANESE
k
l
MALAY
n

and so on.

This variation makes a good homework task and allows everyone to bring in their own individual work the next day.

COMMENTS

Some students may not know how to spell their names in the Roman alphabet—see 5.9.

5.2 Scripts

LEVEL 2–4; children

TIME 25 minutes (possibly for homework)

MATERIALS Dry transfer lettering (such as Letraset) and stencils; small pieces of paper

LANGUAGE Simple autobiographical sentences, for example, 'I like dancing'

PREPARATION Type out several different sentences which include the word 'I', one on each piece of paper. There should be ten more sentences than there are students in the class.

PROCEDURE 1 Ask each student to choose a piece of paper with a sentence on it which says something they empathize with.

2 Each student copies this sentence three times on the same sheet of paper, the first time using transfer letters, the second time using a stencil, and the third time in their own handwriting.

3 The students should display their finished writing on the wall.

COMMENTS 1 This is a much more testing activity than it might seem to be. Even the transfer part of the activity requires the students to internalize the shapes of the letters and then identify them on the transfers.

2 It also helps the students to grasp the vital point that the Roman alphabet can be represented in a very wide range of fonts.

5.3 My own labels

LEVEL 2–4; children (and adults)

TIME 10 minutes per day

MATERIALS Large sheets of paper, articles supplied by students (see below)

LANGUAGE Writing on labels

PREPARATION Tell each student to bring an article of clothing or piece of personal property with English words on it to class each day.

PROCEDURE	**1** Give each student a sheet of paper and ask them to copy their sample of English writing as exactly as possible on to the sheet.
	2 When this is done, the sheets should be displayed on the wall.
	3 Repeat each day with each student bringing a new piece of property to class (for example, watch, pen, book, clothing, walkman, battery, etc.). Gradually, each sheet will come to represent a student's lifestyle.
VARIATION	Rather than using sheets of paper, this can be a page in a student's scrapbook. (See 10.6, 'Scrapbook ideas'.)
COMMENTS	**1** Children in particular should be encouraged to copy the whole sample, including any illustrations.
	2 One purpose of this activity is to give the students a familiarity with the wide range of different ways in which Roman script is written. This is a particularly important part of learning to read English.

5.4 Writing from left to right

LEVEL	**2–3; adults and children (particularly good for right-to-left mother-tongue writing systems)**
TIME	**15 minutes**
MATERIALS	**None, but see Variation 2**
LANGUAGE	**Words being learnt in class**
PROCEDURE	**1** Write three or four capital letters on the board. Each student chooses one and copies it down.
	2 Write three or four lower-case letters on the board. Again, each student chooses one, but it must make a possible combination with the first letter chosen. (You can allow very anxious students to check for acceptable combinations with you.)
	3 Continue writing up three or four letters at a time. The students try to complete words. Each time they complete one, they start a new word (using a capital letter).
VARIATION 1	You can dictate the letters instead of writing them on the board.
VARIATION 2	For learners at the pre-writing stage, either distribute plastic alphabet sets and let them make the words with the plastic letters or ask each student to make themselves a set of alphabet

cards with transfers or stencils, which they then use to make the words.

VARIATION 3   See the next activity for a version of this activity with words.

COMMENTS   The students learn a great deal incidentally about the possibilities of letter combination in (spelling) English words. Learners with non-Roman alphabet mother-tongue writing systems also learn a lot about the cursive nature of writing from this letter-by-letter method of writing words.

5.5 Word by word

LEVEL   3–4; adults and children (particularly good for students with right-to-left mother-tongue writing systems)

TIME   20 minutes

LANGUAGE   Three-sentence stories

PREPARATION   Write a very simple two- or three-sentence story (it could be a simple version of a story in the news). Think of two alternatives for each word or morpheme in the story.

PROCEDURE   1 Write the first word and two alternatives on the board. Each student chooses one and writes it down. So if you write, 'The', 'A', and 'An', a student might choose 'The'.

2 Write three more words on the board. Again, each student chooses one, but it must make a possible combination with the first word chosen.

3 Continue writing three words (or morphemes, for example, *-ed*, *-s*) at a time. The students try to complete sentences. Each time they complete one, they mark it with a full stop and start a new sentence (using a capital letter).

VARIATION 1   You can dictate the words instead of writing them on the board.

VARIATION 2   See the previous activity for a version with letters rather than words.

COMMENTS   The students learn a great deal about the possibilities of word combination in English from this simple, decide-and-copy activity. For example, if a student chooses 'The' initially, and then a countable noun, they will be able to add *-s* if they want a plural. In this way, the students teach themselves a lot about constituent structure without the teacher having to (try to) explain anything.

5.6 Easy to write, not so easy to write

LEVEL	1–2; adults and children
TIME	20 minutes
MATERIALS	Alphabet chart (optional)
LANGUAGE	Names and shapes of the letters of the Roman alphabet

PROCEDURE

1 Explain that you will dictate the alphabet two letters at a time and that the students should write them down, not in the order in which they are dictated, but by writing the easiest letter first. If you think it necessary, either display an alphabet chart or allow the students to have a chart in front of them.

2 Dictate the alphabet two letters at a time, i.e. first 'a, b', then 'c, d', and so on.

3 When you have finished dictating the alphabet, ask pairs of students to compare their versions of the alphabet and discuss in their mother tongue the problems they encountered in forming Roman alphabet letters.

VARIATION 1

As the students get better, you can dictate three or four letters at a time and depart from the order of the alphabet.

VARIATION 2

For students with right-to-left first-language handwriting systems, tell them to write the easy letter from left to right and the harder letter from right to left (i.e. at the right-hand end of the line). After the dictation is over, they 'correct' all the right-to-left letters by writing them from left to right.

VARIATION 3

You can also dictate pairs of words. Choose words which are similar enough in written form to encourage the students to think about why some letters are more difficult than others to write.

COMMENTS

1 Students with a non-Roman alphabet whose first language has a right-to-left writing system will find the first stages of writing the Roman alphabet particularly challenging.

2 This activity also provides familiarity with the names of the letters.

5.7 Crosswords

LEVEL   1–2; adults and children

TIME   15 minutes + homework

LANGUAGE   Roman alphabet representation of students' names

PROCEDURE   1 Print your name in capital letters on the board.

2 Choose a student whose name contains at least one letter in
common with yours and ask them to say their name. Either write
it or, preferably, ask the student to write it on the board in such
a way that it makes a crossword with your name. For example:

3 Continue until all the students have written their names on the
board in a vast crossword. It works best if you allow the students
to choose when to come and write.

4 Either in class or for homework, ask the students to remake
the crossword so that their own name is written horizontally in
the centre, and all the other names make the most compact
crossword they can devise.

VARIATION   As the students progress, you can use this activity for other
ideas, for example, each student can make crosswords of their
family members' names, their own interests, the places they have
visited for holidays, etc. This variation is obviously also suitable
for those who do have Roman alphabet mother-tongue writing
systems, and the results make good diary/scrapbook entries (see
Chapter 10).

COMMENTS   This is a fun activity. The remaking part is especially important
as it gives the students practice in looking carefully at the script
as they make decisions about which words to write where.

Acknowledgement

This simple, brilliant idea was thought up by Anna Korea.

5.8 Shapes and sounds

LEVEL 2–4; children and adults

TIME 40 minutes

MATERIALS Sets of consonant symbols (see Preparation)

LANGUAGE Roman alphabet and the sounds associated with letters

PREPARATION Prepare one set of consonant symbols for every four students, and one set for yourself, on card if possible. Use lower-case letters. The symbols required are:

b, c, ch, d, f, g, h, j, k, l, m, n, ng, p, ph, qu, r, s, sh, t, th, v, w, x, z.

PROCEDURE 1 Group the students in fours and distribute a set of symbols to each group. Ask each group to separate the symbols into five or six sets which have similar shapes. When each group has agreed on the sets, each learner should copy the letters.

2 While the groups are at work, make a wall display of your set of letters, according to their manner of articulation. Your sets will therefore be:

stops: p, b, t, d, c, k, g
fricatives: f, ph, v, th, sh, s, z, h
affricates: ch, j, x (word internally and word finally)
nasals: m, n, ng
glides: w, y, qu
liquids: l, r

(This list ignores the difference between voiced and voiceless 'th', and the sound of 's' in 'measure'. With children, it is better to treat fricatives and affricates as one class.)

3 Tell the students that your sets are not arranged by shape. Ask them to guess how they are organized. Help by making the sounds of the letters in each set.

4 Help the students to become aware of the relationships between sound and letter shape by repeatedly practising the sounds with you.

5 Ask each group to return to their seats and say their letters aloud.

VARIATION 1 You can repeat the activity, this time arranging your letters by place of articulation:

Bilabials: p, b, m, w
Labio-dentals: f, ph, v
Interdentals: th
Alveolars: t, d, sh, ch, j, n, l

Palatal-alveolars: ng, r, s, z, y
Velars: c, g, k, qu, x
Glottal: h

VARIATION 2

You can do the same for vowels, but this is much more difficult as there is so much variation in vowel sound representation in English.

VARIATION 3

Instead of arranging their letters by shape, ask students who have learnt the Roman alphabet to group letters according to the two-letter vowel + consonant combinations such as '-at' or '-in' which can follow them. Thus, b, c, e, f, etc., are a group because they can all precede '-at' to make a word.

VARIATION 4

Instead of making letters, you can work with children's plastic alphabet sets if you have access to them.

COMMENTS

1 This activity gives students a good deal of confidence in both forming letter shapes, and thinking about how and where the sounds are made. So you are helping your students to associate shapes with sounds.

2 This activity works with what we might call a 'pedagogic phonology'. Although a phonetician would no doubt quarrel with treating 'qu' ([kw]) as a glide and 'x' ([ks]) as an affricate, it makes good sense from a pedagogic or instructional perspective at this stage.

3 If students are not familiar with the sounds of the letters in the Roman alphabet, prepare a fidel chart as in 5.9.

5.9 Transliteration

LEVEL

2–3; children and adults with a common non-ideographic first-language writing system such as Arabic or Cyrillic

TIME

30 minutes

MATERIALS

Parallel fidel chart for English/mother tongue (see Preparation)

LANGUAGE

Roman alphabet representations of students' names

PREPARATION

If you do not know the students' mother tongue, you will have to find a bilingual to help you. Prepare a chart in which the letters of the English alphabet are matched with the symbols of the mother-tongue writing system which have the same sounds. (Sometimes parallel alphabet charts can be found in phrasebooks and published beginners' materials. If you can find one of these it will save you time.) Make a copy of this chart for each student.

PROCEDURE

1 Distribute the charts and ask each student to write their name using the Roman alphabet. As the students finish, they should help each other. Very ambitious students can go on to writing their home towns in Roman characters.

2 When everyone has completed this task, go round making suggestions as to conventional ways of spelling the names in English. For example, if a student is called 'Mahmoud', he is very unlikely to have produced this in Roman characters unless he has already had practice. And in the case of place names, English frequently has an Anglicized version which is clearly different from the mother-tongue form.

COMMENTS

1 This is a much harder and more involving activity than you might think. If you know no Arabic, imagine trying to write your name in Arabic script with a chart such as the one prepared for this activity.

2 Although a lot of preparation is involved, once prepared the materials can be used time and again and are very helpful indeed to the students.

Acknowledgement

I first realized how interesting and problematical an activity this is when I had the experience of transliterating my name into Hebrew script in an activity devised by my colleague Arthur Brookes.

5.10 Flash dictation

LEVEL

2–4; adults and children

TIME

20 minutes

MATERIALS

Flash cards (see Preparation)

LANGUAGE

Vocabulary fields such as sports, furniture, fruit, etc.

PREPARATION

Choose a topic and think of 20 vocabulary items. For example, for sports, you might think of football, athletics, tennis, etc. Make one flash card (i.e. a card with the word written on it) for each vocabulary item.

PROCEDURE

1 Show the students the flash cards you have made and write the vocabulary items on the board.

2 Explain that you will flash the cards briefly in front of the class one by one. The students should write each word as you flash it.

3 Flash the 20 cards up one after another. Do not say the words written on them.

4 Allow the students time to compare their results before flashing the cards up more slowly a second time while the students 'correct' their original dictations.

As well as working in vocabulary fields, you can use any set of vocabulary items that are appropriate, such as the words in a text that the students are to read or work on next.

1 When you choose a category like sport or furniture, remember to take the students' level into account. For example, most of the sport words are international so you can work with them at level 2. But with clothes, the words will mostly be new.

2 Kenneth Goodman claims that reading is 'a psychological guessing game' in which 'look and say' skills are very important. This activity gives practice in real reading of this kind because you are working with familiar items and not allowing time for the students to use phonic methods. This will often mean that some students are much more successful than others.

5.11 Recognizing familiar words

2–4; adults and children

20 minutes

Words that occur in English and the mother tongue

1 Write 10 to 12 words which occur in both languages on the board. Likely examples include football, theatre, television, telephone, music, cassette, coffee, whisky, ballet, metro, park, orchestra, pianist, police, airport.

2 Ask each student to copy the words down in the order in which they recognize them.

3 Ask each student to copy the words down in the order of ease of pronunciation.

4 Ask the students to compare their lists with each other.

5 Set aside a little time for providing a pronunciation model.

Ask the students to order the list according to the number or proportion of words with similarly formed letters to the letters of their mother-tongue writing system.

COMMENTS   This is a useful activity for drawing the students' attention to the similarities and differences between their mother-tongue writing systems and Roman script.

Acknowledgement

This is a variation on one of Branka Grundy's clever ideas for teaching Cyrillic script to learners of Russian.

6 More words

In one sense, lexis is prior to syntax, at least as far as language learners are concerned. One can communicate messages quite effectively even with single words. In fact, in emergencies we all do it with the single word 'Help!'. For this reason, we should ensure that our students are acquiring vocabulary as fast as possible in the early stages of learning. After all, we first select our chosen words from the lexicon and then combine them in grammatical sequences.

Some points about vocabulary:

1 There are a number of myths one frequently hears even from teachers. The most common is that a learner can only acquire eight or ten words in an hour. Yet the educated native speaker of English knows the meanings of getting on for quarter of a million words. So if it were true that one could only acquire vocabulary at the rate of eight or ten words an hour, this would make language learning a painfully slow process.

2 Many words that we feel to be quite common are in fact relatively infrequently used. The COBUILD project has shown that a word like 'apple' is typically used only once a fortnight by native speakers. And since the notion of frequency of use is not salient to a language learner anyway, this would seem to be a doubtful criterion on which to base the vocabulary we decide to teach.

3 Although they know the meanings of getting on for quarter of a million words, educated native speakers of English still only know the meanings of fewer than half the words in the language. And of course we are all the time forgetting words and learning new ones. This suggests that linguistic competence should not be measured by volume of words acquired or securely retained.

4 In our mother tongues we rarely learn new words either at first meeting or by knowing the equivalent token in some other language. In reality we acquire vocabulary by frequently encountering words in a variety of contexts. And we frequently have only a hazy and sometimes even a completely wrong idea of what a word means. In fact, you do not need to have a conscious knowledge of what a word means to use it appropriately: how many native speakers of English could give a convincing account of the meaning of the word 'the', for example?

5 There is a very great deal of evidence to show that words are stored in some logical, economical way in the mental lexicon. We all do this sorting for ourselves, but it may be that language learners are helped when they encounter words that are to some extent sorted into groups. (See activities 6.1, 6.2, 6.3, 6.5, 6.7, and 6.8.)

6 Even more amazing than the fact that we can learn the meanings of quarter of a million words is the fact that we can combine these words with each other meaningfully. Indeed, sometimes we even get new meanings which are not the sum of the two collocated words but something more or different: so that when we talk about 'a short book', we do not mean a book which is only ten centimetres high. Nor is its opposite 'a tall book'.

Taken together, these points suggest that we acquire vocabulary at a phenomenal rate, but that we do not acquire items in isolation or at a stroke. Vocabulary items are learnt progressively and in context.

In addition, even native speakers frequently feel the need for a dictionary. In the same way, your learners will need both bilingual and monolingual dictionaries: a bilingual dictionary because they will sometimes need to work from one language to the other, and a monolingual dictionary to enable them to learn more about the words in English that they are acquiring. They will probably be happiest with a good children's dictionary (such as *The Oxford Children's Dictionary*), or a good intermediate learner's dictionary (Oxford *Wordpower* is good) to begin with. Later, they will graduate to a more advanced (learner's) dictionary (Longman and Oxford are both good). (See activities 6.2 and 6.3.)

There has been a great deal of interest in dictionaries in recent years and a very wide range of dictionary types is now available. So a dictionary like COBUILD, which is based on meaning as determined by environment, may well be founded on the soundest principle available in modern lexicography. This does not necessarily mean, however, that the entries will be the most informative for learners, or that such an approach will better Webster's excellent 'formal plus functional' definition strategy. (See activities 6.10 and 6.11.) So, some combination of different dictionaries will probably be ideal for most learners. And we cannot be many years away from a computerized dictionary capable of providing every kind of information that a user might require as well as automatically updating itself and altering its own entries.

The thirteen activities in this chapter recognize the importance of words in the early stages of learning. As you will find, they present a very eclectic set of approaches to the acquisition of second language lexis.

6.1 My area

LEVEL   3–4; adults and children

TIME   30 minutes

LANGUAGE   Semantic fields such as body parts, pleasure, etc.

PROCEDURE   1 After your students have made a certain amount of progress, ask them to work individually or in pairs and consider the areas or headings they would need to classify all the vocabulary they have learnt. Allow five to ten minutes and use the board to bring together categories. Try to encourage the students to be imaginative, so that you end up not only with concrete categories like animals and body parts, but also abstract notions like pleasure and pain.

2 When you have established a number of areas, ask the students to volunteer to be responsible for an area each.

3 Once you have a keeper of each vocabulary area, allow a further 10 minutes for the students to start making a wall display that will feature all the items in their area. Encourage them to use all sorts of ways of presenting their vocabulary, including pictures, charts, family trees, etc.

4 Explain that each student will be responsible for adding further items to their area as new words occur in class or in private reading.

Acknowledgement

This idea was thought up by Nic Sinclair of UCLES when he was following an MA course at Durham.

6.2 Making a dictionary 1

LEVEL   2–4; children and adults

TIME   30 minutes per session

MATERIALS   Colour magazines, scissors, glue, blu-tack, bilingual dictionaries

LANGUAGE   New words

PROCEDURE   1 Distribute colour magazines and ask each student to cut out three pictures of items which they cannot name in English but would like to. Each should be mounted on a piece of paper and either blu-tacked to the wall or displayed on the desk.

2 Ask the students to circulate looking at the pictures. Where they think they know the English word, they should suggest it to the person who cut the picture out. While this is going on, make a list of all the English words yourself and write them on the board.

3 Ask the students to use their dictionaries to check the words on the board. When they find the right English word for each of their pictures, they should write it on the paper on which the picture is mounted.

4 When all the pictures have been matched with the words on the board, the class should order them alphabetically and either make a wall display or put them in a folder for future reference.

COMMENTS

This activity encourages the students to think about using their dictionaries out of class for self-instruction purposes.

6.3 Making a dictionary 2

LEVEL

3–4; children and adults

TIME

20 minutes in class + homework

MATERIALS

Monolingual or bilingual dictionaries

LANGUAGE

Names, clothes, sport, etc.

PREPARATION

Prepare one category for every two students. Good categories include English forenames, sports, clothes, fruit, furniture, animals, food, entertainments, drinks, and other superordinate categories.

PROCEDURE

1 Write the list of categories on the board. Tell the students to find a partner and choose a category. Make sure that each pair has a different category.

2 Tell the pairs to begin to make a list of words in their category that begin with each letter of the alphabet. They should try to get as close to finding a word for each letter as possible.

3 This activity should be finished for homework and the completed entries displayed on the walls.

CONTINUATION 1

Once these 'dictionaries' are displayed on the walls, encourage the students to circulate, studying them and adding other examples.

CONTINUATION 2   Ask the students to re-order the dictionaries so that alphabetical order is replaced by ordering according to some other criterion, such as how good a member of the category each item is or how enthusiastic the student feels about each item.

COMMENTS   Encourage the use of dictionaries in this activity. This is particularly important as the dictionaries will be used to check that putative English words really are correct.

6.4 Matchbox city

LEVEL   2–4; children (and adults); class or group size up to 10

TIME   Any number of 20–25 minute sessions

MATERIALS   A model town which can be constructed out of components such as is sold under the 'Matchbox' trademark. Toy cars and people if possible

LANGUAGE   Directions, shopping, emergencies, etc.

PREPARATION   Take a model town set to class.

PROCEDURE   1 Make the model town set available and ask the students to construct a town with it.

2 Ask a student to give directions to get from one part of town to another—for example, from the post office to the station. Prompt as appropriate.

3 Once the model is established, let the students take turns at asking for and giving directions.

VARIATION 1   Any number of activities are possible with a model town set. They include shopping, planning visits, staying with someone, driving (parking, reversing, etc.), emergencies, community living, accidents, writing to local residents about proposed road works, etc. All these activities quickly lead into role play.

VARIATION 2   The layout can be changed from time to time by mutual agreement—this involves negotiating and a good deal of instruction giving.

VARIATION 3   You can also dictate new layouts or modifications to the existing layout.

COMMENTS

Realia of this sort help the students to visualize a context in which language would occur. It is also very interesting to see how naturally the students move from acting as though they were outside the world they have created to acting within it in a natural role play. It is ideal if the town layout can be left on display in the classroom so that the students can return to it periodically during a sequence of lessons.

6.5 I quite like . . .

LEVEL

2–4; adults and children

TIME

25 minutes

LANGUAGE

I really/quite/don't like [food]

PROCEDURE

1 Pair the students. Tell them that you are going to give a list of items and each student must decide for each one if their partner really likes it, quite likes it, or does not like it.

2 Choose a category, for example food, and give the first item, perhaps 'pizza'. If a student thinks their partner is very enthusiastic about pizza, they write down 'I really like pizza'; fairly enthusiastic 'I quite like pizza'; or unenthusiastic 'I don't like pizza'.

3 Continue until you have mentioned 10 types of food.

4 The students rejoin their partners and give each other the lists of likes and dislikes. Allow five minutes while the students tell each other how well they predicted each others' tastes.

CONTINUATION 1

As the students get more proficient, introduce four-, five-, and six-point scales and negative expressions like, 'I hate . . .'.

CONTINUATION 2

Introduce sub-categories, like vegetables, within a category like food. This provides more specialist vocabulary.

COMMENTS

1 With very early stage learners, you can supplement the vocabulary items with pictures.

2 Try to choose vocabulary which meets the language needs of your students. If, for example, they are shopping for themselves in an English-speaking country, use items that they will find in the supermarket.

6.6 All the things I own

LEVEL	2–4; adults and children
TIME	30 minutes
MATERIALS	Bilingual dictionaries
LANGUAGE	I own [number + article(s)]; every week I eat [number + food items]
PROCEDURE	1 Write up a number of frames on the board. Good examples include:

I own . . .
Every week I eat . . .
Each week I buy . . .

2 Ask each student to choose one of these and write an autobiography which takes the form, 'I own one car, two watches, three pens . . .', etc. Allow the use of bilingual dictionaries.

3 Completed biographies should be displayed on the wall and can be used as the basis for further work—including question and answer work, survey work, etc.

CONTINUATION 1 Once a student has their own autobiography, he or she can use the same categories and make guesses about other members of the class.

CONTINUATION 2 As the students progress, a similar activity can be used for teaching frequency. For example, 'Each month I visit the hairdresser once, the cinema twice . . .'.

6.7 The best thing about . . .

LEVEL	3–4; children and adults
TIME	25–30 minutes
MATERIALS	Colour magazines (optional)
LANGUAGE	Vocabulary that describes things the students are enthusiastic and unenthusiastic about
PROCEDURE	1 Say 'travel' and tell the students to write down the best and the worst things about it. They should use English if possible, but otherwise may write down mother-tongue words.

2 Continue dictating topics and allowing time for the students to write down the best and worst things about each topic. Good topics include sport, my house, television, winter, night-time, Britain, friends, lovers, my job, Christmas. Ten topics should be enough.

3 Encourage the students to compare answers with their neighbours and use dictionaries to translate any mother-tongue words into English.

4 If you wish, make lists for a wall display. This can also be illustrated with pictures from colour magazines.

CONTINUATION

As the students progress, you can suggest that they use phrases or give several different sub-areas within a topic area. For example, you can suggest travel by car, by bus, by train, etc.

6.8 Adam and Eve

LEVEL

1–4; children and adults

TIME

20 minutes

LANGUAGE

Paired expressions like 'egg and bacon', 'cat and dog'

PREPARATION

Make a list of 10 to 12 paired expressions. Good examples include fish and chips, sun and moon, day and night, gin and tonic, Saturday night and Sunday morning, bread and butter, black and white, salt and pepper, oranges and lemons, cup and saucer, brother and sister, mum and dad, indoors and outdoors, town and country, long and short, bed and breakfast.

PROCEDURE

1 Dictate the first member of the pair. The students should write down what they think the whole pair should be.

2 When you have given all the starters, ask the students to compare answers. Check that the class has the right answers.

COMMENTS

You can ask one of the students to be responsible for collecting further pairs that occur and adding them to an ongoing wall display. From time to time, you can ask the students to decide which pairs they think go together best.

6.9 Have you got . . .?

LEVEL   2–4; adults and children

TIME   15 minutes per pair of pictures

MATERIALS   Paired pictures

LANGUAGE   Have you got [x] in your picture?

PREPARATION   You will need a pair of pictures for every 6 to 10 students. Each picture in a pair should have similarities but must not be identical. Good pairs include pictures of the ingredients of a recipe and the finished dish, pictures of similar rooms, etc.

PROCEDURE   1 Divide the class into groups of 6 to 10. Ask each group to further divide into two halves. Distribute one of the pairs of pictures to each half of each group.

2 Tell the students to ask each other 'yes/no' questions for five minutes. Each half-group should take it in turn to ask a question.

3 After five minutes, tell each half-group to draw the picture they think the others in their group are holding.

4 Allow time for the groups to compare drawings and pictures.

COMMENTS   The similarity helps the students a lot. They realize that their picture and the other picture are similar, and this prompts the questions they ask.

6.10 Real words?

LEVEL   3–4; adults

TIME   6–8 minutes for each pair of words

MATERIALS   Dictionaries (monolingual if possible)

LANGUAGE   The phonology of possible words in English; necessary vocabulary; 'a thing for . . .', 'someone who . . .'

PREPARATION   Choose a number of words which you want your students to learn, preferably vocabulary which they are about to need for classwork. For each word, invent a non-existent paired word which has either one letter more or one letter less. The words you invent must be impossible English words phonologically. For example, if the real word was 'month', you might invent 'pmonth'.

PROCEDURE

1 Write the pairs of words on the board. Explain that one word in each pair is a real word and the other does not exist. Tell the students that they should decide which are the real and which are the invented words.

2 Each student looks up the word they think is the real one in their dictionary and writes its meaning down. If they look up the invented word first, then they look up the real word next.

3 Each student should invent a meaning for each invented word. The meaning should be expressed in English, perhaps using formulas like, 'a thing for . . .' or 'someone who . . .'.

4 Go round the class checking that everyone knows the meanings of the real words. Then allow the students to tell each other the meanings they invented for the non-possible words.

COMMENTS

The valuable part of this activity is the stage where learners have to guess. Their intuitions are usually very accurate, and this gives them a sense of satisfaction—they have learnt to recognize the phonology of English words even if they do not know the meaning of the word in question.

6.11 Extending vocabulary

LEVEL

1 and 2; adults

TIME

3–5 minutes per vocabulary item

MATERIALS

A collection of the everyday objects your learners need to be able to talk about, such as a toothbrush, a pair of socks, a pair of scissors, a watch, a pen, etc.

LANGUAGE

Wh- questions; materials; countries; actions

PREPARATION

1 Take twice as many everyday objects to class as there are students.

2 Prepare four prompt cards and write one of the following questions on each:

What's it made of?
Where does it come from?
What's it for?
What is it?

PROCEDURE

1 Hand the four prompt cards to one of the students and ask them to choose an object whose English name they do not know.

2 The student should read out the first question: 'What's it made of?' for a classmate to answer. The student continues with the other three questions. (You may have to supply some of the vocabulary items needed to answer the questions.)

3 Ask a second student to take the prompt cards, and then repeat Step 2.

VARIATION

Ask each student to bring an object to class and keep it hidden in their bag. Each student takes a turn at saying what the object is made of, where it comes from, and what it is for. The other students guess what it is (in their mother tongues if necessary).

COMMENTS

1 With classes of more than 10 students, ask the class to work in groups of four to five and make a set of prompt cards for each group.

2 Notice that each question practises a different area of vocabulary:

Materials: it's made of wood/metal/glass/plastic/cotton
Countries: it comes from Italy/Japan/Britain
Actions: it's for writing/cutting/telling the time

3 This activity also helps students to classify English nouns as countable, uncountable, and dual.

4 This makes a good activity if repeated each day, as the vocabulary items become progressively more familiar and the class become correspondingly more fluent. Once the students understand the activity, it is a good idea to ask them to bring in any of their own objects whose English names they want to know.

5 The questions are also realistic: they are the kind of questions the students will need to ask when they go shopping and the kind of structures they will need when talking about objects with other people.

6.12 'To' dictation

LEVEL	1–4; children and adults
TIME	15 minutes
MATERIALS	A simple story or set of sentences (see Preparation)
LANGUAGE	Identifying particular words chosen by the teacher
PREPARATION	Write a simple story or series of sentences. Each sentence should contain a particular word of your choosing. Good words include 'I', 'the', and 'to'.
PROCEDURE	1 Explain that you are going to dictate a simple story in which each sentence will contain one instance of the same word. Tell the students what the word is, and explain that they have to listen for this word and write down the position that it occupies in each sentence. For example, if the students hear 'I like to drink coffee' and the word they are listening for is 'to', they simply write the number '3'.
	2 Dictate the story at what you judge to be the appropriate speed.
	3 Allow the students time to compare their answers before dictating the story for a second time.
VARIATION	This activity can also be done without telling the students which word to listen out for. They must identify it themselves.
COMMENTS	This dictation obliges the students to retain each sentence and then carry out a process on it. In one respect, this is more difficult than simply reproducing the sentence as in traditional dictation.

6.13 Cartoon jigsaws

LEVEL	2–4; adults and children
TIME	4 × 5 minutes
MATERIALS	A cartoon; access to photocopier if possible
LANGUAGE	Description of a picture or cartoon
PREPARATION	Choose a cartoon with a lot of drawing in it. (Newspaper cartoons are often too simple.) Enlarge it to A3 size if possible

and cut the photocopy into four pieces. These may be equal sizes (i.e. cut the cartoon diagonally) or cut so that each piece contains a distinct part of the cartoon. If possible, try to cut it so that the key to understanding the joke is all within one 'key' piece.

PROCEDURE

1 Hold up the simplest piece of the enlarged cartoon and ask the students to provide the vocabulary for what they see depicted. Help where necessary. Display the piece of cartoon on the wall or board and continue the lesson with another activity.

2 After 20 minutes, hold up the second simplest piece of the cartoon and repeat Step 1.

3 After 20 minutes, hold up the third piece of the cartoon and repeat Step 1.

4 After a further 20 minutes, insert the key piece of the cartoon into the wall display, but so that it is reversed and the students only see the blank side of the paper. They then guess what is on the other side. Help as necessary and try to guide the students to guessing the point of the cartoon.

VARIATION

This activity is a variation of the familiar jigsaw activity in which each member of a group has a different piece of a cartoon and the students obtain information from each other in an attempt to reconstruct the whole picture.

COMMENTS

1 Good cartoons are those where each of the cut up parts contain some common items such as trees, a dark sky (= night), etc. This makes it possible for students to start confidently with each new piece and also to guess the 'key' piece more successfully.

2 You may find the cartoon below useful:

7 Firsts

This chapter has been given over to 'firsts' to remind us that language learners typically have the sense that they pass a number of landmarks in their attempts to learn a second language. The more of these the members of your class experience, the greater their sense of progress, and the greater their consequent motivation. For these reasons, it is a good idea to point out whenever a particular type of activity (such as listening comprehension or video watching) is a 'first'.

The activities are arranged so that those that require little or no material resources are at the beginning of the chapter, while those that require technology are at the end.

7.1 First mime

LEVEL

1–4; adults and children

TIME

30 minutes (+ 20 minutes for optional Step 4)

LANGUAGE

Descriptions of action in the present tense

PROCEDURE

1 Divide the class into groups of four to six. If you are working in a class with several mother tongues, the groups should be made up of students with a common first language if possible.

2 Explain that each group has 10 minutes to devise and practise a short mime. They should use their mother tongues to do this. While the groups are rehearsing, observe them carefully and make sure that you can describe what is going on in simple English.

3 Ask the groups to take turns at presenting their mimes. As each group presents, provide a commentary in simple English.

4 (Optional) Return to one of the groups and ask them to perform again while the other students draw a simple cartoon strip depicting the mime with your commentary as captions. (Allow an extra 20 minutes.)

VARIATIONS

There are other activities for which you can provide commentaries or voice-overs, such as a group drawing on the board, a mother-tongue drama, certain games, mother-tongue story writing, mother-tongue story-telling, model making, do-it-yourself, cooking, etc.

COMMENTS

These activities match language and action, with the teacher supplying the former and the students the latter. As the students become more proficient, they can begin to provide the language as well as the action.

Acknowledgement

These ideas are based on suggestions made by Brian Tomlinson.

7.2 First autobiography

LEVEL

2–4; children and adults

TIME

25 minutes

LANGUAGE

I was born in . . .; I live in . . .

PROCEDURE

1 Write sentence starters such as 'I live in . . .', 'I work as . . .'/ 'I'm a . . .' on the board. (Do not include 'My name is . . .'.)

2 Tell the students that they should write their own autobiography in exactly 25 words, not a word more or less.

3 The finished autobiographies should be displayed on the wall with a sheet of paper underneath each. Ask the students to read each one and write the name of the person they think wrote it on the sheet of paper.

VARIATION 1

Instead of Step 3, ask the students either to display their autobiographies on the wall together with any matching drawings or photographs and/or add them to their scrapbooks (see 10.6, 'Scrapbook ideas').

VARIATION 2

The students can write about themselves in the past, present, or future.

VARIATION 3

The students can write about other members of their families, or about their classmates.

COMMENTS

The exact word limit is very important as this provides a stimulus for careful rewriting or editing so make sure that it is strictly adhered to.

7.3 First traveller's tale

LEVEL	3–4; adults
TIME	30 minutes
LANGUAGE	Description of a journey

PROCEDURE

1 Ask each student to think of a journey they have made. Any journey is fine, from travelling half-way round the world to walking up the road to the shops, so long as there are one or two interesting features of the journey worth describing. The students should think in their mother tongues.

2 Once the students have all got a traveller's tale worked out, ask them to make a map of the route, marking in all the features along the route, and particularly the interesting ones worth describing.

3 Group the students in threes and ask them to show each other their maps and describe their journeys in English.

4 When the groups have finished, ask one or two groups to choose a map and story to describe to the whole class.

COMMENTS

This technique can be transferred to other activities and is important in its own right: the students start with a meaning which they have fully explored in their mother tongue and then translate it into English via a pictorial representation.

Acknowledgement

The idea of a map-based story is Gerry Kenny's.

7.4 First test

LEVEL	2; children and adults
TIME	20 minutes
LANGUAGE	Providing short answers to *wh-* questions

PREPARATION

Prepare 20 to 25 questions that can be answered with information the students have already learnt. Possible questions might include

What wakes you up in the morning?
What do you call the meal you eat in the evening?
Which number comes before 10?
How many toes have you got?
What must you take with you when you visit another country?

PROCEDURE

Give out the question papers and allow 15 minutes' answering time.

VARIATION

At a slightly more advanced level, supply the answers (for example, 'with a comb'), and ask the students to write the questions.

COMMENTS

1 You will need to decide how to 'mark' this test. With adults, you will probably want the class to supply the answers and mark their own papers.

2 This is a test not of syntactic knowledge but of real-world knowledge and the students' ability to express it in English. This is a very important principle of authentic testing.

7.5 First in-class questionnaire

LEVEL

2–3; children and adults

TIME

30 minutes (+ 20 minutes for optional Step 3)

LANGUAGE

and so is [Maria]'s; and so does [Maria]

PREPARATION

Prepare a simple questionnaire which asks for information about the likes/interests/hobbies of the students. All the areas should be ones which you have already practised so that filling in the questionnaire will not pose linguistic problems. After each question, add 'and so is', or 'and so does' as appropriate. Your questionnaire might look something like the example opposite (if you had worked in the areas it asks about). Make a copy for each student.

PROCEDURE

1 Distribute copies of the questionnaire and allow the students time to complete the left-hand column in each question.

2 Tell the students to circulate, trying to fill in the 'and so is/does' part with the names of fellow students with the same likes/interests/hobbies. When they have done this, they should consider who is most like them in the class.

3 (Optional) Get the class to make a diagram showing how all the members of class are linked according to who thinks someone else is like them.

WHO'S LIKE ME?

1 My star sign is _____ and so is _____'s

2 My favourite time of day is

_____ and so is _____'s

because _____

3 My favourite day of the week is and so is _____'s

_____

because _____

4 In _____ I _____ and so does _____

5 I really like _____ and so does _____

_____ and so does _____

_____ and so does _____

6 I'm a _____ and so is _____

7 I feel happy when _____

_____ and so does _____

8 I get angry when _____

_____ and so does _____

and when _____

_____ and so does _____

9 I like to spend the evening

_____

_____

_____ and so does _____

10 I'm good at _____

_____ and so is _____

11 I'm no good at _____

_____ and neither is _____

12 I think the best way to learn

English is _____

_____ and so does _____

The person most like me in the class is _____

COMMENTS

1 This is a very involving activity to take part in and the results are very revealing. Students often find that they have a great deal in common with other students who seem quite unlike them superficially.

2 One of the keys to making the first in-class questionnaire a success is to ensure that the parts the students fill in do not pose language problems. Ideally, they should be revising and collating language which they have already learnt and used earlier in class.

7.6 First street survey

LEVEL   3–4; adults

TIME   75 minutes (can be spread over two or three lessons)

MATERIALS   Large sheets of card or paper such as A3; native speakers

LANGUAGE   'Yes/no' and *wh-* questions

PROCEDURE   1 Tell the students that they will be conducting a survey outside the classroom. First, they will have to choose a topic to investigate. It is a good idea to suggest possible topics such as clothes, watches, achievements in the past year, plans for the next year.

2 Once the students have chosen a topic, they should invent the questions they want to ask. If the chosen topic was watches, typical questions might include

Did you buy your watch or was it a present?
How much did it cost?
How old is it?
Does it keep good time?
What do you feel about your watch?

As the class agrees each question, write it on the board and ask each student to copy it down, leaving room to write in the answers provided by two people. Six or seven questions should be enough.

3 When everyone has a copy of the questions, explain that the students will be going out of the building in pairs to interview people. Each student will conduct two interviews. The non-interviewer will approach the informant and say, 'Excuse me, we're students learning English. Can my friend ask you some questions about . . .? It'll take just one minute.' Allow 20 minutes for the interviews and set the time by which everyone must be back in the classroom.

4 Ask the students to work in groups of about 10 and collate all the information they have obtained. Give out large sheets of paper or card so that the findings can be represented in diagrammatic form and displayed on the walls.

5 When the wall displays are complete, get the students to tell you about their results.

COMMENTS

If the only native speakers readily available are in the building you are working in, allow the students to canvass them. Obviously, this activity can only work if you are in a native-speaker environment or close to hotels, an airport, a university, or an institution where there are potential informants who speak good English.

7.7 First fable

LEVEL

3–4; adults and children

TIME

30–40 minutes

MATERIALS

Simplified fables (see Preparation)

LANGUAGE

'There was once' and other typical examples of the genre

PREPARATION

Make four or five simplified versions of well-known fables, each reduced to three or four sentences. Try to make sure that together they contain a variety of the language associated with fables.

PROCEDURE

1 Display your prepared fables on the wall and read each aloud, making sure that the class understands them.

2 Ask the students to work in groups of three or four and give them a choice of themes to construct original fables about. Good topics include successful language learning, the progress of beginners, and the value of speaking a second language.

3 Each group should present what they have written, preferably by reading and performance.

4 Display the fables on the wall.

VARIATION

This activity also works well if you give the groups the 'Moral', rather than the topic at Step 2, and then ask them to construct fables to illustrate it.

7.8 First reading comprehension

LEVEL   1–4; adults and children

TIME   15 minutes

MATERIALS   See Preparation

LANGUAGE   Simple text chosen by the teacher

PREPARATION   Choose or write a simple text which describes a simple object. Type the text in such a way that it resembles the object. For example:

```
This is my tab
le lamp. I bo
ought it on ho
liday in Italy
. The shade i
s peach colour
ed and the bas
       e is
      made
  of pink an
  d green ma
  rble. I li
  ke it a lot!
```

Photocopiable © Oxford University Press

Make copies for the students.

PROCEDURE   1 Distribute copies of the comprehension and give the students five minutes to puzzle it out. Allow the use of dictionaries.

2 Ask for volunteers to read it aloud.

VARIATION   As the students become more proficient, they can design picture comprehensions for each other. It is important to check that the English is correct first.

COMMENTS   This seems a very simple activity, but in fact it requires the students to hold an image of the text in their minds which does not correspond in a one-to-one way with the image on the paper. So although the students may be misled into thinking they are merely reading, they are in fact reconstructing a memorized image in a new way.

7.9 First postcard

LEVEL
2–3; children and adults on a course away from home in an English-speaking country

TIME
20 minutes

MATERIALS
A postcard for each student

LANGUAGE
I am having a good time; I have been to . . .

PREPARATION
Either buy a postcard for each student or arrange an opportunity for them to buy their own. A supply of stamps is also a good idea.

PROCEDURE
1 Ask each student to think of someone to whom they would like to send a postcard written in English.

2 Provide several sentence starters for the students to choose and complete. Good examples include

I am learning . . .
I have been to . . .
I hope you . . .

Encourage the students to work with your starters until they get to the last sentence, which should be an original sentence of their own invention. They may want to make first drafts of their messages before completing the postcards.

VARIATION
More ambitious is the first cassette. This is challenging at beginner level and requires time. But if you ask the students to talk a little about themselves, perhaps including some of the information provided by them in other lessons, and even to sing a song, they will be surprised to find how much they know. This can be done individually or in groups. Good group/class projects include making a cassette to send to a twinned institution in another country or as an end-of-course souvenir to summarize all they have learnt.

COMMENTS
The value of this activity lies in providing the students with an opportunity to show someone outside the language class that they are making progress.

7.10 First group presentation: seasons

LEVEL   3–4; children and adults

TIME   20–30 minutes a day preparation time for three or four days + 30 minutes' presentation time

MATERIALS   Magazines and coloured pens or pencils

LANGUAGE   Description of seasonal weather, behaviour, etc.

PROCEDURE   1 Ask the students to form four groups: spring, summer, autumn, and winter. Each student joins the season that their birthday falls into.

2 Explain that the groups will have three (or four) planning sessions in which to prepare a presentation about their season. The presentations will be a mixture of pictures (which may be taken from magazines) and words (which the group will prepare, with your help).

3 Go round helping the groups by giving them sentence starters such as 'In [season], we . . .', 'In [season] everything . . .'. Encourage each group to work with black and white pictures, colouring them in and learning language (from you) as they do this. Stress that every season has its characteristic weather, routines, foods, moods, illnesses, etc.

4 Sit back and enjoy the presentations, which may be turned into wall displays or even be recorded and left available for individual listening later.

VARIATION   A simpler (or preparatory) activity involves giving each group a black and white seasonal picture and asking them to colour it in. Distribute a single set of coloured pens or pencils to the whole class so that one group will have to ask another for the colour they want.

COMMENTS   1 One reason for choosing this theme for the first group presentation is that everyone has lots of knowledge readily available and will therefore be encouraged to try and display it in English. It is very important for the teacher to be as much of a language resource as possible.

2 If you have students from both northern and southern hemispheres in your class, you will have to decide how to manage the fact that the seasons fall in different months. The simplest way, if you have enough students, is to make a display for each hemisphere.

Acknowledgement

Anna Korea has an activity based on seasons which is less demanding than this (but more elaborate than the Variation).

7.11 First extended story

LEVEL	3–4; adults and children
TIME	Days 1 and 2, 5–7 minutes; Day 3, 30 minutes
MATERIALS	Text of a short story (if possible three or four copies)
LANGUAGE	Simple, repeated structures

PREPARATION

1 Choose a very short, simple story written for pre-school native-speaker children. Fairy tales, folk tales, stories with a lot of repetition are ideal. The 'Mr Men' series is particularly suitable.

2 If possible, choose a story for which you can also obtain a cassette read by a professional reader or actor. Otherwise, make a tape yourself.

3 Provide a guided listening handout, with the first two or three sentences given in full, followed by key phrases from the rest of the story.

PROCEDURE

Days 1 and 2

Play the tape, but not as part of the lesson—for example, while the class is walking between classroom and cafeteria or during break-time.

Day 3

1 Prepare a board diagram: either draw key moments in the story, or, if the story includes movement from one place to another, write a chain of key words to link the locations, or choose whatever other form of diagram is appropriate to the story and will facilitate listening.

2 Distribute the guided listening handout and go through it with the students.

3 Play the tape, pointing to the relevant parts of the handout and the board diagram. Mime appropriate parts of the story. Be prepared to play the tape twice if the class wants you to.

4 Distribute as many copies of the original text of the story as you have and ask each group with a text to sit in a circle. Play the tape again and ask each student to listen to two sentences with the text in front of them before passing it to their neighbour, indicating as they do the place in the text which the tape has reached.

CONTINUATION

You can follow up by working intensively on part of the story or you can ask the students to retell the story in their own words.

COMMENTS

There are several pre-listening, preparatory and support elements to this 'first'. This is because an extended text of this sort will stretch the beginners to the very limit.

7.12 First newspaper

LEVEL

2–4; adults

TIME

35 minutes

MATERIALS

One newspaper for every four students

LANGUAGE

Understanding the topics of newspaper stories

PROCEDURE

1 Group the students in fours and distribute one newspaper to each group.

2 Tell the students to share out the group's newspaper amongst themselves. Working individually, each student skim-reads as many stories as possible. If they understand the gist of a story, they write under it 'This story is about . . .'. Allow 15 minutes for this.

3 Ask the students to work together in their groups and try to understand any stories that any individual has been unable to understand. If they are successful, they write under the story 'This story is about . . .'.

4 Ask each group to choose the most interesting story someone in their group has come across, cut it out, and display it on the wall.

VARIATION 1

Other good first newspaper experiences include

- asking the students to find a story they think other students in the class would understand. The selections are then circulated for each student to read. The students keep a list of the stories they read and understand, writing after each story 'I read a story about . . .'
- asking each group to make a list of the name of everything they can understand in a newspaper, appealing to you for the name of the feature where they are uncertain. So each group's list would be likely to include page numbers, football scores, temperatures, pictures of famous people, masthead, date, names of products advertised, phrases such as 'Dear Sir', etc.

VARIATION 2

Some of the ideas for working with newspaper pictures in *Resource Books for Teachers: Newspapers* are also suitable for early stage learners.

COMMENTS

Newspapers are a very important classroom resource because teenage and adult beginners already bring knowledge of how to read them from their first language. They therefore allow you to build on existing skills. If you choose tasks that beginners can succeed in, they have a real sense that they are making progress and are already beginning to do the things people do in the real world.

7.13 First listening comprehension

LEVEL

3–4; adults and children

TIME

30–40 minutes

MATERIALS

A line drawing of the inside of a room; access to a photocopier; tape recorder

LANGUAGE

Simple sentences with the structure 'noun phrase–copula–prepositional phrase'

PREPARATION

1 Either make a simple line drawing of the inside of a room or find one from a book or enlarge the example below:

Photocopiable © Oxford University Press

Make a copy for each student.

2 Make a descriptive recording, spoken very slowly indeed, of the room's furnishings in the following way: 'The typewriter is

on the desk. The trays are on the desk. There are two telephones on the desk.' Make sure that your description moves round the room in a clockwise direction.

PROCEDURE

1 Distribute copies of the drawing and ask the students to supply the names of any items of furniture that they know. Supply the names of the other items yourself. The students should write the names of each item on the drawing of the item in the picture.

2 Play the tape two or three times.

3 Ask the students to repeat any of the sentences that they can remember. As you gradually reconstruct the tape in this way, encourage the students to write the prepositions in the most appropriate places in the picture.

4 When all the students have written all the prepositions on the picture, play the tape for the last time. Encourage the students to join in with the tape and describe the room as the tape is being played.

CONTINUATION

Encourage the students to make their own line drawings of a different interior—their own room, a shop, an office, or whatever. They should also write their own scripts and record them. This works well when you divide a class into groups and each group has the task of making a listening comprehension for another group. This might even be the class's first English project.

7.14 Watching the first video 1

LEVEL

3–4; adults and children

TIME

30 minutes

MATERIALS

1–2 minutes of off-air video

LANGUAGE

Simple, emotional dialogues

PREPARATION

1 Choose one to two minutes of video, preferably from a well-known soap which members of the class are likely to have seen before. The passage you choose should contain emotional material, a declaration of love, or a quarrel, for example. The language should be reasonably simple.

2 Choose six to eight simple sentences from the video, such as 'Oh God, I love you!' or 'I'll be your wife' or 'I'll be your girlfriend, I'll be your mistress or I'll be anything in between'.

3 Copy each sentence on to a separate slip of paper and make enough copies for each student to get one sentence.

PROCEDURE

1 Give each student a slip of paper with a sentence written on it.

2 Ask the students to circulate. Each time two students come together they say their sentences to each other with the appropriate feeling. When most students have said their sentences to each other, ask them to return to their places.

3 Explain that you will play the video without sound. Each student should try to identify where their sentence comes.

4 Repeat Step 3, but this time ask the students to wave their slips of paper when they think their sentence is being spoken.

5 Play the video with sound.

VARIATION

Another good first watching activity is to find ten seconds of video which are entirely predictable from the preceding minute. Typical examples include violent scenes, accidents, and romantic moments. Show the video up to the predictable moment and ask the class to predict what will happen next. When the class has guessed what will happen, ask four or five questions about it which the students should answer in writing. Typical examples for an accident might be:

Will he fall backwards or forwards?
Will the first or the second woman fall over him?
Will the dog bite his left leg or his right leg?

Then play the video. The purpose of this activity is to make the students concentrate really hard on understanding and rapidly processing a very short stretch of video in English.

COMMENTS

This is a very satisfying 'first'. The students will have

- practised speaking a sentence with genuine feeling, with several different classmates
- correctly identified their sentence's place in a video by lip-reading
- understood English-language television successfully for the first time.

Acknowledgement

Gerry Kenny first demonstrated the paper-waving technique to us at a Pilgrims trainers' seminar when he was showing us how to make pop songs accessible to our students.

7.15 Watching the first video 2

LEVEL

3–4; children and adults

TIME

20–25 minutes

MATERIALS

Video extracts and scripts

LANGUAGE

Simple sentences chosen by the teacher

PREPARATION

Choose a short extract (about 45 to 60 seconds) of off-air video in which someone is speaking reasonably slowly and full face to the camera. It is important to choose a passage where the students can lip-read what is being said. Soaps like *LA Law* are particularly good for this sort of extract and have the added advantage of being well-known to most learners. Make a transcription and copy it for each student.

PROCEDURE

1 Distribute scripts. Play the video through twice while the students follow the script.

2 Play the video again and encourage the students to mouth the words as they are being spoken.

3 Play the video twice more with the students ·speaking the words chorally with the actors.

4 Turn the sound off and play the video again with the students speaking the words chorally again. Encourage the students to work without their scripts if possible.

5 Play the soundless video two or three more times with individuals trying to speak the words with the actors, if possible without scripts. Encourage members of the class to add any corrections.

COMMENTS

1 If you have chosen a passage where it is possible to lip-read, this will encourage the students to dispense with the scripts. Once the sound is turned off, it is no longer possible both to follow the script and remain synchronized with the actors.

2 Although a certain amount of preparation is required for this activity, it is very confidence-boosting for the students, particularly when repeated regularly.

3 If there is an English-language television programme available locally, it is a good idea to use this as a source of material. This enables the students to begin to watch it with some confidence.

7.16 First CALL session

LEVEL

3–4; children and adults

TIME

30–40 minutes

MATERIALS

A computer with a word processing programme for every four students

LANGUAGE

Recognizing cohesion and coherence in stories

PREPARATION

Choose or write three very simple stories, each about 10 sentences long. All the stories must contain the same number of sentences. Type the first sentences of each of the three stories into the computer, followed by all three second sentences, and so on. Copy the stories on to the other computers.

PROCEDURE

1 Divide the class into groups of four and ask each group to work at a computer. Teach the students how to delete sentences.

2 Explain that there are three stories on their disks. Each group should read the three first sentences and decide which story to follow. Once they have decided, they delete the two first sentences which they did not choose.

3 The group should continue deleting two out of every three sentences to make a coherent story.

4 Each group reads its story aloud and the other groups indicate if they are unhappy about the sentences chosen.

VARIATION

Good first CALL lessons for those with word-processing skills include completing and redesigning a form, and designing an invitation to an event such as a language performance of some kind.

COMMENTS

1 One of the advantages of working with word-processing packages is that the students get satisfaction from using the programme successfully and this makes their language achievements seem more incidental and natural.

2 There are many brilliant ideas in Hardisty and Windeatt's *CALL*, in this series, several of which are adaptable for beginners.

8 Games

You and I know what games are from our experience of them in real life. Real games reflect underlying human cultural and psychological frames. These include wanting to win, contests in which one tests oneself in order to perform at a higher level than an opponent, characteristic routines understood by the members of the group who play them, the idea that each 'side' or team member will get a turn, stages where one part of the game is a preparation for the next part, systems for measuring success, and calculation of risk. Often games are transparent rehearsals for life. It is for these reasons that games are the most serious classroom activity.

It is therefore odd that so many language teachers use the word 'game' to describe an activity that is felt to be less serious, even less important, than regular lessons. In general, classroom games have accepted the thesis that we learn through play but have failed to appreciate the importance of games in our lives.

In this chapter, games are treated as more important than mainstream classroom instruction. Each of the activities mirrors the routine of a well-known game, which is described at the beginning of the activity. In selecting games to work from, I have tried to choose those that recognizably satisfy the frames described in the first paragraph. Thus, the first activity in the chapter is based on the children's game, 'Hide and seek', in which one person hides and the others try to find them. This game is clearly a vestige of the time when we were hunters, with the one who hides being the hunted and the seekers being the hunters. In this sense, it represents the trace memory of a fundamental human experience. 'Hide and seek' also involves wanting to win. It is a contest (is my hiding place superior to yours?) in which one tests oneself (how small/dark/airless/ uncomfortable a place can I squeeze myself into?). There are teams of seekers. 'Hide and seek' has a routine understood by members of the group who play it (including giving someone time to hide, indicating when the seeking starts, and looking in various places ritualistically). 'Hide and seek' allows each player a turn, with success in the previous round sometimes seen as a qualification. And it involves calculation of risk (if the curtains do not move, the seekers will never find me, but if they do . . .).

The first three activities in this chapter are based to some degree on hiding and seeking; the next four, activities 8.4 to 8.7, are based on games which reward speed and skill; activities 8.8 and 8.9 test the ability to plan and calculate; and the last activity in the chapter, 8.10, reminds us that the consequences of being the focus of attention can be what players seek to avoid.

8.1   Hide and seek

'Hide and seek' is a game in which one person hides and the others try to find them.

LEVEL

3–4; children and adults

TIME

35 minutes (or homework + 20 minutes of class time)

MATERIALS

Class readers

LANGUAGE

Adjectives and adverbs that collocate with existing text

PREPARATION

List two adjectives and two adverbs for each student. These must be different for each student. Each list of four items should be written on a separate piece of paper.

PROCEDURE

1 Allocate a different page of the class reader to each student and give each of them one of the four-word lists.

2 Tell the students to look through their page of the reader for a suitable place to add or 'hide' just one of their four words. When they find a suitable place, they should copy out as much of the page as they have time for and include their own word in its chosen place. (This step can be set as a homework task.)

3 Ask the students to pass their texts to their neighbours. Each student underlines the word they think is the hidden word in the text in front of them and then passes it one place further round the circle.

4 Repeat Step 3 as many times as appropriate.

5 Allow time for the 'hiders' to see what words were 'found' in their texts.

8.2 Battleships

'Battleships' is a game in which each player hides their ships on a board where each square is numbered (for example, A3, G1, etc.). The players take turns at naming a square and each hopes to hit the other player's ships.

LEVEL

2–4; children and adults

TIME

30 minutes

MATERIALS   Two 'boards' for each player (see Preparation)

LANGUAGE   Short sentences chosen by the students

PREPARATION   Make two 10 × 10 grids, as below. It is better if both grids are
on the same piece of paper. Make a photocopy for each student.

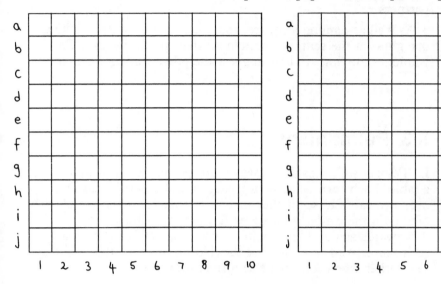

Photocopiable © Oxford University Press

PROCEDURE   1 Each student hides the words of a five-word sentence
containing a minimum of 20 characters and a maximum of 30
characters on one of their grids. All the words must be written
horizontally from left to right. Before the sentences are written
on the grids, check spelling and grammar.

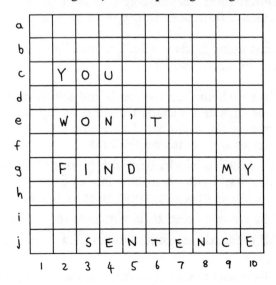

2 Pair the students. They should not show each other their
grids. Each student takes it in turn to name a square (for
example, A1, D9, etc.) on their partner's grid. As each square is
named, their partner must say whether there is a letter on that
square, and, if there is, which letter. The students should use
their second grids to record the information they get from their
partners.

3 As well as naming a square, each turn also consists of taking
one guess at the sentence written on their partner's grid. The
winner is the first student to guess the other student's sentence.

8.3 Pelmanism

In 'Pelmanism', a pack of cards is spread out face downwards on
a table. Each turn consists of trying to find a pair by turning
over two cards to see if they match. If a player is successful, they
take both the cards; if unsuccessful, they turn them face
downwards again. This quickly becomes a test of memory as
each player tries to remember the 'hiding place' of the card they
saw earlier when someone else turned it over.

LEVEL	**3–4; children and adults**
TIME	**30 minutes**
MATERIALS	**Card index cards are ideal, otherwise use squares of paper**
LANGUAGE	**Writing: short autobiographical sentences;** **Speaking: sentences in the form 'It was x who . . .'**
PREPARATION	If card index cards are not available, prepare two squares of paper for each student.
PROCEDURE	1 Give each student two cards and tell them to write their name on one card and a short, true, interesting sentence about themselves on the other. Check grammar and spelling before the sentences are written on the cards.

2 This activity works best with groups of around 10. If you have
a big class, divide them into smaller groups at this stage. The
rest of the instructions apply to each group.

3 The students read their sentences to the group.

4 All the cards are collected, shuffled, and placed face down on a
table.

5 The students take it in turns to turn two cards face upwards
and read them aloud. The purpose is to match a sentence with

the name of the student who wrote it. When a student turns over two matching cards, they say 'It was [name of student] who said [sentence on card]' and take the two cards. You will need to help with this model sentence. The student who collects the most cards wins.

VARIATION 1

(Groups of 4–6)

Write three sentences on three separate cards for each student in the class. Each sentence should contain a different colour word. Give each student their three-sentence cards together with three more blank cards. The students copy the colour words on to their new cards. All the cards are turned face down and the game commences (see Step 5 above). You can also use numbers, animals, countries, etc. as key words.

VARIATION 2

(Groups of 4–6, 15–20 pairs)

Prepare cards which the students will recognize as pairs when they turn the right two cards over (for example, 'fish and chips', 'egg and bacon') or 'couples' cards (for example, 'Laurel and Hardy', 'Robin Hood and Maid Marian'). Variations on this theme with goalkeepers and football teams, countries and currencies, etc. are also possible.

VARIATION 3

(Groups of 4–6, 15–20 pairs)

Prepare cards so that the first member of the pair contains a single word and the second contains a sentence with a gap which the single word can fill. You can use a syntactic category that is more grammatical than lexical, such as prepositions, for this form of 'Pelmanism' too. Alternatively, the sentences can be lines of poetry or lines from nursery rhymes. Often such lines allow you to have a self-evident pairing. For example, 'four' must be the missing word in:

One, two, three, . . ., five
Once I caught a fish alive.

With couplets, if you gap the last word in one of the lines, rhyme will be the guiding principle in finding the right pairing of word and sentence.

8.4 Snap

'Snap' is played with a pack of picture cards that usually have three or four examples of each design. Each player turns their top card face upwards simultaneously. If two identical cards are exposed, the first player to say 'Snap' takes all the cards that have been turned up since the last time 'Snap' was called. The loser is the player who ends up with no cards.

LEVEL	**1–4; children and adults**
TIME	**40–50 minutes**
MATERIALS	**A reader and eight card index cards or small squares of paper for each student**
LANGUAGE	**Sentences chosen by the students from their readers**

PROCEDURE

1 Group the students in threes.

2 Give each student a reader and eight card index cards. Tell the students to choose eight different sentences from their readers and copy each on to one of their cards. They should be careful not to let the other members of the group know which sentences they have chosen.

3 Each group is now ready to play 'Snap'. The first time the class does this, choose one of the groups to demonstrate with.

4 Each player turns their top card face upwards simultaneously. The first member of the group who thinks they can see a similarity between the three sentences says 'Snap' and explains what the sentences have in common—this must be a word or a meaning or a theme (i.e. it cannot simply be a sound or a sequence of letters). If the other members of the group accept the explanation, the person who said 'Snap' takes all the cards. If the explanation is not accepted, or if no one says 'Snap', then the next three cards are turned up. The winner is the student who ends up with the most cards.

VARIATION 1

You can make simpler versions of 'Snap' using colour or number words.

VARIATION 2

A good version of 'Snap' for those learning Roman script is to make a letter pack repeating each lower-case letter twice. Use a standard 52-card pack of playing cards and stick an address label with a letter on it on to each card. Play with two to four players. The aim is to say 'Snap' whenever two of the exposed cards have letters with descenders or ascenders.

8.5 Racing demon

'Racing Demon' is usually played by a single person. The game starts with seven piles of playing cards, with one card in the first pile, two in the second, three in third, etc. The top card of each pile is placed face upwards. There should therefore be 28 cards in the piles and 24 left over.

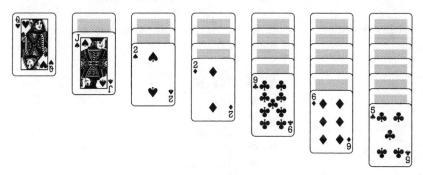

If any two top cards are consecutive numbers of different colours (for example, Q♥, J♠, and 6♦, 5♣), the card with the lower number is placed on the higher. The next card under the card that moved is now turned face upwards.

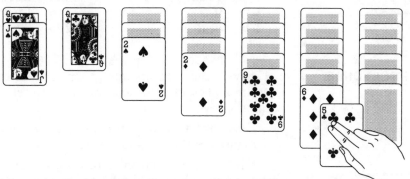

The remaining 24 cards are now turned over one by one. Each time a card of a different colour and one point lower in value than any of the top cards on the piles is turned over, it is placed on that card. So, if the first card you turn over is 10♥, it is placed on J♠. (This would allow 9♣ to be moved to 10♥, and the card under 9♣ to be exposed.)

The purpose of the game is to collect all four suits, Spades, Hearts, Diamonds, and Clubs, starting with the ace of each. So if the second card you turn over is A♠, you can begin your collection of Spades and take 2♠ off its pile and expose the card under it.

Once you have turned over all 24 cards, you may turn over those you have left again. Sometimes 'the Demon comes out' (i.e. all four suits are collected); more often it does not.

One last rule: if there are no cards left in any pile, a king may be moved to the empty space.

LEVEL	3–4; children and adults
TIME	30–35 minutes
MATERIALS	One pack of cards for every four to five students
LANGUAGE	Adverbs, sentence adverbs, conjunctions; simple sentences that make a continuous story

PREPARATION   Either write the following key on the board or make a copy for each student:

A	♥	When	A	♦	Quickly
K	♥	But	K	♦	Silently
Q	♥	And	Q	♦	Thoughtfully
J	♥	Because	J	♦	Gently
10	♥	Although	10	♦	Naturally
9	♥	In order to	9	♦	Anxiously
8	♥	However	8	♦	Wearily
7	♥	So	7	♦	Excitedly
6	♥	While	6	♦	Loudly
5	♥	Just as	5	♦	Sweetly
4	♥	Then	4	♦	Lovingly
3	♥	If	3	♦	Luckily
2	♥	And then	2	♦	Slowly

PROCEDURE

1 Divide the students into groups of four or five. Give each group a pack of cards and ask them to set up 'Racing Demon', i.e. the seven piles of cards.

2 Explain that each group is to play 'Racing Demon' and demonstrate the rules of the game.

3 Explain that every red card exposed represents the word given in the key. Thus, in the following arrangement Q♥ represents 'And', 2♦ represents 'Slowly', and 6♦ represents 'Loudly'.

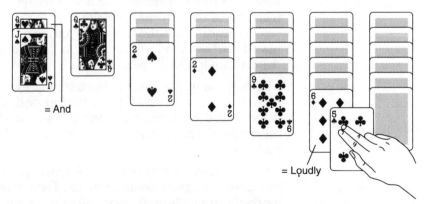

= And
= Loudly

Make sure that everyone understands all the words in the key.

4 Explain that each time a black card is placed on top of a red card, the group must make a sentence beginning with the word associated with the red card. As each story develops, it should make sense. All the members of the group should remember all the stories they are making.

VARIATION 1

If you have a cassette recorder, encourage any group that has a good story to record it.

VARIATION 2

The stories can be written down as they are being made up—this is both an aid to memory and provides a permanent record of stories which will slowly disappear as 'the Demon comes out'. A written version also enables you to help the students to improve or correct their stories later.

COMMENTS

You sometimes get a bizarre effect when one story is transferred to another. (This might happen if a sequence with 7♥ at the top was moved to 8♣—which could happen if 7♦ had been under 8♣ and was added to the Diamond suit that was being collected.) You have to decide whether to allow bizarre sequences—they can be fun—or whether to get the group to re-write the last part of their story to make it consistent.

8.6 Egg and spoon

In 'Egg and spoon' races, children try to run as fast as possible while balancing an egg on a spoon. The egg must not fall off.

LEVEL

1–4; children and adults

TIME

15 minutes + 10 minutes the next day

LANGUAGE

Sentences at the limit of the students' comprehension

PREPARATION

You will need a set of sentences of increasing complexity from three to ten words long. It is best to use variations on sentences that you have already used in class. If this is difficult, a possible set might be

He likes fish.
She eats French cheese.
The student went to London.
The old lady bought a present.
When I was young, I liked chocolate.
My friend saw the film at the cinema.
Did you know the girl who won the race?
I travelled where I wanted for more than a year.

PROCEDURE

Day 1

1 Say the first sentence and ask the students to repeat it together after you.

2 Explain that you are going to say more sentences and that each will get longer. The students should say them together after you but stop at the first one that they cannot repeat correctly. Say the sentences slowly one after another until no one is repeating them after you.

3 Tell the students that they should remember the sentence before the one that they did not repeat accurately. Explain that you will say them again so that the students can identify and remember their sentence. Make it clear that they must remember it without writing it down.

Day 2

Ask the students to write their remembered sentence down. They should team up with other students who had remembered the same sentence to make sure that they have all remembered it correctly.

CONTINUATION

Do this activity every day for a week or two with sentences that are useful in a real context, such as shopping.

COMMENTS

1 It is difficult to give the quite complicated instructions for this activity so it may be a good idea to do a rehearsal and then repeat it again with new sentences. If you have a class reader, you can take sentences from it. Lower-level students may need an explanation in their mother tongue.

2 This is the 'egg and spoon' race of language learning, the linguistic equivalent of carrying an object you can barely balance over a considerable distance. Although it seems a simple activity, it is a very stretching one.

8.7 Word scrabble

'Scrabble' is a board game in which each player has a number of letters, some or all of which they try to order so as to make complete words.

LEVEL 2–4; children and adults

TIME 30 minutes

MATERIALS A 'Word scrabble' set (see Preparation) for every six students

LANGUAGE Text from a reader rearranged into shorter sentences

PREPARATION 1 Take a text of approximately 150 words—the class reader is ideal. Make one photocopy for every six students, enlarging the original. Cut each text up into individual words and put each set into an envelope.

2 Make a 'Scrabble' board. To do this, take a large sheet of paper and rule 18 lines one way and 25 the other. Make one copy for every six students. Mark a central square as the starting square.

PROCEDURE Distribute one 'Scrabble' set to every group of six students. Play 'Scrabble' by the usual rules:

1 Each student gets seven words.

2 The first student tries to make a phrase or sentence using as many words as possible; he or she takes new words from the envelope to replace those used and scores one point for each word used.

			the	soldiers	came				

3 The students take turns at this, making sure that their phrase or sentence includes part of another phrase or sentence. If a student cannot make a phrase or sentence in this way, they may exchange some or all of their words for new words from the envelope. They score one point for each word used, including any words in existing sentences to which they add a new word or words. They may only add new words at the beginning or end of existing sentences or where the words are added at right-angles to an existing sentence.

			the						
			prisoner						
			saw						
			the						
		the	soldiers	came					
			through						
			the						
			window						

4 Continue until all the words have been used up and no one can make any new sentences or phrases. Add the scores, taking away one point for each unused word anyone has left.

COMMENTS

1 In many games we have to balance what we can achieve against the opportunity it may give to an opposing player. In the original version of 'Scrabble', if one player makes a singular noun and another can merely add -*s* to it to make it plural, that second player will score one point more than the first player who had done the hard work of thinking out the original word. So before I make such a word, I have to calculate the consequences. In this version of 'Scrabble', the sentences one player makes will enable the next player to make their sentences too.

2 There is a junior commercial version of 'Scrabble' which is suitable for level four beginners.

8.8 Pontoon

The purpose of 'Pontoon' is to amass up to five cards whose face values add up to no more than twenty-one. Each player starts with two cards and then has the option of taking more from a face-down pack in an attempt to get as close as possible to twenty-one. Any player who goes over twenty-one is automatically eliminated. The winner is the player who has five cards whose face values add up to twenty-one or less; if no one has five cards, the winner is the person who gets closest to a score of twenty-one.

LEVEL

2–4; children and adults

TIME

The first time you play, 50–60 minutes; other times, 25–30 minutes

MATERIALS

One pack of playing cards and 52 address labels or squares of paper and glue for every 10 students (if you have more than 10 students, make sure that each additional pack of playing cards has a different pattern on the back so they do not get mixed up)

LANGUAGE

Simple sentences (e.g. he was very tall, she stood beside the chair) linked to make a story; counting practice

TEACHER PREPARATION

For the first time you play 'Pontoon':
1 Make a copy of the following list of 52 sentences. (If you have access to a photocopier, this will save you a lot of time.)

he loved her	he was well dressed
he loved her	she was well dressed
he really loved her	he was wearing glasses
she thought he loved her	she was wearing glasses
she loved him	he spoke to her
she loved him	she spoke to him
she really loved him	he was smiling at her
he thought she loved him	she was smiling at him
he was her older brother	he was very tall indeed
he was her younger brother	she was very tall indeed
she was his older sister	he was wearing brown shoes
she was his younger sister	she was wearing black boots
he spoke softly	he stood beside the table
she spoke softly	she stood beside the chair
he looked intelligent	he laughed as he spoke
she looked intelligent	she laughed as she spoke
he was tall	he was looking straight at her
she was tall	she was looking straight at her
he was handsome	he thought she had beautiful lips
she was beautiful	she thought he had beautiful eyes
he was smiling	he was wearing a denim jacket
she was smiling	she was wearing a tweed jacket
he was very tall	he wondered what her name was
she was very tall	she wondered what his name was
he was very handsome	he was sipping his champagne slowly
she was very beautiful	she was sipping her champagne slowly

2 Cut the copied list up so that each sentence is on a separate slip of paper. It is a good idea to put the slips straight into a small box to make sure that you do not lose any of them.

CLASS PREPARATION

For the first time you play 'Pontoon':
The first time your class plays 'Pontoon', they will need to make the cards which you can use every time you play after that. Although this may seem a bit of a chore, the class should do the preparation as this makes it easier to explain how to play the game later on.

1 Each student must take a playing card (if there is more than one pack, one card from each pack), an address label or square of paper and glue for each card, and a sentence. They copy the sentence on to the label and stick it to the front of the playing card(s).

2 When a student has finished a card/cards, they bring the card(s) to you, put the slip which they had copied in the waste-paper basket, and take the materials to make another card.

PROCEDURE

1 Divide the class into groups of 10. Appoint a controller for each group.

2 Explain that
– the controller will begin by dealing two cards to each player
– each player will have the chance to take more cards
– each card contains a three-, four-, five-, or six-word sentence
– the purpose of the game is to make a story with the sentences written on the cards, which may be arranged in any order. The maximum story length is 21 words. Any player with a longer story will be eliminated
– the winner is the student who has a five-card story no more than 21 words long; if no one has a five-card story, the winner is the student who gets closest to a 21-word story with three or four cards.

3 The first time you play, choose a student to demonstrate with. Let us imagine our chosen student is called Rosa. Begin by asking the controller to deal two cards to her. Imagine Rosa gets

he was her younger brother
he was handsome

4 She must now decide whether she wants another card. Presumably she does (she only has eight words so far), so she says 'yes please' and the controller gives her a third card. Imagine this card says

she was wearing glasses

5 Rosa has

he was her younger brother
he was handsome
she was wearing glasses

She must now decide whether she wants a fourth card. Presumably she does (she only has 12 words so far), so she says 'yes please' again and the controller gives her another card. Imagine this one says

she stood beside the chair

6 Rosa now has

he was her younger brother
he was handsome
she was wearing glasses
she stood beside the chair.

As she has 18 words, she would be foolish to ask for another card, so when the controller offers her a fifth card, she says 'no thank you'.

7 Rosa now waits to see what will happen to the other students—maybe her 18-word story will win. Meanwhile, she arranges her four cards in the best possible order to make a story, perhaps:

she stood beside the chair; he was her younger brother; he was handsome; she was wearing glasses.

COMMENTS

You can always alter some of the cards to give extra interest each time you play this game. Your students will often have suggestions too.

8.9 Street furniture Rummy

'Rummy' is a card game in which each player is dealt a 'hand' of cards. Players may exchange one card for another to improve their hands. The winning player is the one who can arrange all their cards in sequences of at least three numbers of one suit (e.g. 7♥, 8♥, 9♥ or 10♣, J♣, Q♣), or in sets of at least three examples of the same number (e.g. 5♦, 5♣, 5♠).

LEVEL

2–4; adults

TIME

20 minutes +

MATERIALS

A specially prepared pack of cards for every 12 students; address labels or paper and glue

LANGUAGE

The main station, the post office, a telephone box

PREPARATION

1 Take one pack of playing cards for every four students. It is possible for students to play in teams of two or even three, so that one pack can be sufficient for eight or even twelve students.

(Nor is it necessary for the whole class to be involved in this activity at the same time.)

2 Write down 17 three-word phrases, each of which should describe a feature of the average town. The following phrases may be useful: the main station, the bus depot, the new shopping centre, the railway bridge, the high street, the public park, the savings bank, a public lavatory, a building society, a recreation centre, a swimming pool, a telephone box, a pedestrian crossing, a covered market, a department store, a car park, the traffic lights. Write one word of each phrase on an address label or small piece of paper. Make sure the playing cards are in random order and then stick one address label/piece of paper to each playing card.

PROCEDURE

1 Group the students in fours. One student shuffles the cards and deals six cards to each of the students in the group. He or she places the rest of the pack word-side down on the desk, turns up the top card, and places it beside the face-down pack.

2 The student to the left of the dealer picks up either the upturned card or the top card of the face-down pack—whichever they choose. She or he then lays down a three-word phrase if she or he can make one and discards an unwanted card on the upturned pile of cards.

3 The next student now takes a turn, and so on round the circle. The purpose is to make 2 three-word phrases and thus end up with no cards left in your hand.

COMMENTS

Keep adding new sequences to your pack whenever you come across one in class.

8.10 Sentence Tig

In 'Tig', one child chases another and when the child being chased is 'tigged', they become the chaser.

LEVEL

2–4; children and adults

TIME

35 minutes

LANGUAGE

Adverbs: very, only, probably, often

PROCEDURE

1 Ask each student to think of a true, interesting sentence about themselves. Allow a minute or two and then check that each student has a sentence.

2 Each student dictates their sentence to the rest of the class, who write the sentence down together with the name of the

student who made it up. Give help with the English and make corrections where necessary.

3 When all the sentences have been dictated, write a list of adverbs on the board. Good examples include: very, possibly, probably, only, often, sometimes, occasionally.

4 Start the game yourself by choosing one of the students' sentences and adding one of the adverbs to it. The student whose sentence you had chosen is now 'on' and must choose another student's sentence and add an adverb to it. For example:

Cristina: I send postcards + often
→   *Cristina often sends postcards.*

5 Continue playing until the students weary of the game.

VARIATION   There are lots of possible variations: at Step 3, you can write up adjectives, time clauses, simple 'if' clauses, etc.

9 Interactions

This chapter contains seven activities to give students practice in interacting with the world outside the classroom. Some of the activities involve working with pictures that represent the world. Other activities involve working with people, sometimes passively, sometimes productively.

Obviously, your students can only interact with people in English if you are working in an English-speaking environment, so it may be that some of these activities are not feasible for you. For this reason, the activities are arranged so that those that are rehearsals for real encounters are at the beginning of the chapter and those that involve actual interaction with native speakers are at the end.

9.1 Contexts for phrases

LEVEL	2–4; children and adults
TIME	30–40 minutes
MATERIALS	Colour magazines (optional)
LANGUAGE	Excuse me, Good, Sorry, Can you help me?
PROCEDURE	1 Write a phrase on the board that might be used in several different contexts. Good examples include 'Excuse me', 'Sorry', 'Good', 'Can you help me?', 'Thanks', 'I see', 'Oh dear'.

2 Ask each student to think of two contexts in which they think this phrase might be used. The first should be the context they think everyone else will have thought of, and the second a context they think no one else will have thought of.

3 Ask each student either to draw two pictures or to find two pictures from colour magazines to show how the phrase is used in each of the contexts they have thought of. They should include a speech bubble containing the phrase in their drawing or picture.

4 Display the finished products on the wall, with appropriate and inappropriate examples clearly separated.

VARIATION

This activity also works well if you provide starters which the students complete. Good examples include 'How do I . . .?', 'Could you tell me . . .?', 'Is it possible . . .?', 'Where . . .?'.

COMMENTS

The wall display is very important in this 'rehearsal for the real world' activity. It will show lots of identical uses of a phrase, and then fewer and fewer examples of the less common uses, finally tailing off into non-possible examples. So the display is a mirror of the frequency of usage which the students themselves have created.

9.2 Representing self

LEVEL

3–4; adults

TIME

40 minutes

LANGUAGE

Questions and answers

PROCEDURE

1 Ask each student to write two questions. The first should be a question about themselves that the other students in the class can easily answer. The second should be a question that the other students probably do not know the answer to but could try and guess. They should refer to themselves by their names. For example, the first question might be 'Where does Paola live?' and the second 'Where did Paola buy her jacket?'.

2 Ask each student to take it in turns to ask the class the easy questions. The class answers them orally.

3 Ask each student to take it in turns to ask the class the difficult questions. This time, each student writes their answer down. For example, 'Paola bought her jacket at Benetton'.

4 Each student displays their answers on their desk. The students circulate, looking at the answers to the difficult questions about themselves, changing their names to 'I', and correcting the answers where necessary.

VARIATION	There are lots of possible minor variations. For example, at Step 4 the students can make a list of all the answers to their difficult questions and then re-order them according to how close they are to being correct. Or in a non-homogeneous group, the questions can be about the students' countries.
COMMENTS	Guessing is a very important part of this 'rehearsal for the real world' activity because there will be times when a student wants to give a particular answer but does not know how to say it in English. This means that they have to balance what they want to say with what they can say.

9.3 Describing the street

LEVEL	1–4; children and adults
TIME	90 minutes (can be spread over more than one lesson)
MATERIALS	A photograph or postcard of a shopping street within walking distance of the classroom; tracing paper; access to photocopier
LANGUAGE	There are [cardinal number] shops. The [ordinal number] shop is a shoe shop
PREPARATION	Trace the outline of (some of) the buildings shown in the photograph or postcard. Place the traced outline on a photocopier and enlarge it to A4 size or similiar. Make one copy for each student.

PROCEDURE

1 Show the photograph or postcard to the students and help them to describe it. You can choose your own structures to practise. Appropriate structures include

– there are [cardinal number] buildings/people/windows/storeys
– the [ordinal number] shop is a shoe shop/chemist's/butcher's
– the [ordinal number] shop has [cardinal number] windows/
storeys
– the [type] shop is next to the [type]; the next shop is a [type].

2 Once the class can describe the photograph or postcard, take the students to the street itself to practise the structures they have learnt. At this stage, you can add new vocabulary, for example:

– there are [cardinal number] burglar alarms/stationers
– [cardinal number] shops have bay windows/chimneys.

When the class have practised the structures freely, return to the classroom.

3 Back in the classroom, give out the photocopied outlines and do a picture dictation: you describe the street, while the class draw in the details.

4 When the dictation is over, the students compare their drawings with the photograph or postcard.

VARIATION

More ambitiously, you or your students can make a video of the street and work with that.

COMMENTS

The outline is very important because it enables the students to draw in perspective and to scale.

Acknowledgement

Anna Korea and I thought out and trialled this activity, and Melanie Ellis suggested the Variation.

9.4 Useful things to do in English

LEVEL

1–4; children and adults

TIME

10 minutes per activity

LANGUAGE

This book belongs to . . .

PREPARATION

As it is a good idea to do several of these short activities in which the students use English for a real-world purpose, think up one for each day of the week. Suitable activities include:

– writing 'This book belongs to [name]' inside a book
– labelling files or folders appropriately
– writing a bilingual address label or business card (particularly good for students without Roman script)
– listing one's American or English clothes and shoe sizes
– listing vital words associated with a particular notion such as travel, computers, menus.

PROCEDURE

Set aside 10 to 15 minutes each day to help the students to learn the useful real-world English in each of the five categories you chose.

VARIATION

Encourage the students to make suggestions for simple activities that they would like to be able to do in English. If you are working in a country where English is spoken, these should include several oral activities.

9.5 One-word sentences

LEVEL

1–4; children and adults

TIME

20–30 minutes + occasional further sessions

LANGUAGE

One-word sentences: Yes, No, Help, Please; one-word signs: Toilet, Hotel, Station

PREPARATION

(Optional) Take several pictures containing one-word signs into the class with you.

PROCEDURE

1 Ask the students to think about all the one-word sentences and signs that they know in English. If you have taken pictures into the class with you, begin by identifying the signs in the pictures. As the students get more ideas, let them come and write their one-word sentences or signs on the board. Make one column for sentences and another for signs.

2 Make a wall display of these one-word sentences and signs. Tell the class that you will be returning to this area at a regular time each week, and will be looking for new examples that the students have learnt or noticed to add to the wall display.

VARIATION 1

You can move on to two-word sentences and signs, and then three-word ones. Interestingly, the number of signs diminishes as the number of words grows, but, obviously enough, the number of sentences increases very rapidly indeed as the number of permitted words increases.

VARIATION 2

At Step 2, ask the students to draw illustrations for the one-word sentences with a bubble coming out of the speaker's mouth and the word written in.

VARIATION 3

You can make this a peripheral learning activity if you prefer (see Chapter 10, especially 10.9 and 10.10). If you do this, it is a good idea to start with pictures that include signs.

COMMENTS

1 This activity helps students to recognize what they see written around them and to pay particular attention to it.

2 Even in non-English-speaking countries, there are a very large number of one-word and two-word English signs about. The students will already know what many of them mean.

3 Short sentences are very useful. Students often make the mistake of thinking that native speakers use long ones like 'May I have a ticket to the bus station, please?' when in fact, if they say anything at all, it is either 'Station' or 'Thirty-five'.

9.6 Collecting eavesdroppings

LEVEL

2–4; children and adults

TIME

Day 1: 5 minutes + out-of-class time; Day 2: 20–25 minutes + out-of-class time

REQUIREMENT

You need to be in a country where there is English-language television, preferably some form of drama. Alternatively, you could use a video

LANGUAGE

Language of conversation, speech acts

PROCEDURE

Day 1

Ask the students to watch an English-language play, soap, or sitcom, and listen out for and note down two or three short, idiomatic utterances. For example, 'Good morning' would be at the simple end of the continuum and 'Next time I'll get you' might be at the difficult end. These should be brought to class.

Day 2

1 Ask the students to share their eavesdroppings with the class. Make sure that everyone understands and makes a list of all of them.

2 Tell the students that they should select one of the utterances on their list every ten minutes as they watch English-language

television at home and try to find places where they can say it to one of the speakers in the play. They can also watch local mother-tongue television with the sound off and chip in with the English utterance wherever possible. Tell learners at the top end of the level to remember a place where they felt they used the English especially effectively so that they can tell other students about it in the next class.

VARIATIONS

There are many uses of the eavesdropping technique, but you do need to be in an English-speaking environment to collect them. The simplest is just listening in shops to see how native speakers ask for things. More subtle is listening to conversations to see what language goes with smiling or touching. Sometimes you will want the students to report back in class so that you can follow the eavesdropping up and practise the overheard structure. Here are some eavesdropping suggestions for beginners:

- Listen out for numbers (Day 1), and for numbers and the nouns that follow them (Day 2).
- Listen out for what people say when they ask for things in shops, at table, or in bars and restaurants.
- Listen out for the words that follow a particular conjunction such as 'and' or 'because'.
- Listen out for what people say when they meet each other, or touch, or start a conversation with a stranger, or open a door for someone else.
- Ask the students to make a poem entitled *Overheard* out of their fragments.

COMMENTS

One real advantage of eavesdropping is that the students hear authentic speech acts and idiomatic uses of language and contribute these themselves to the class. This helps them to avoid learning only literal meanings.

Acknowledgement

Alan Maley suggested the fifth variation.

9.7 Using native speakers as listeners

LEVEL 2–4; adults

TIME 30 minutes + out-of-class time

REQUIREMENT An English-speaking environment

LANGUAGE I'm [Ahmad], I come from [Jordan], I'm a [student]

PROCEDURE 1 Provide the students with a model biography of yourself in the following format:

I'm [Peter]
I come from [Durham]
I'm a [teacher]
I've got [two] children and my [wife] is a [teacher too]

2 Ask the students to provide biographies of themselves in four or five sentences like yours. Keep them practising till everyone can represent themselves fluently.

3 Ask the class to help you make a list on the board of all the native speakers of English they expect to meet later in the day. This can include not only people whose names they know, but also people like 'the lady who serves in the cafeteria'. Continue until there are as many native speakers as members of the class.

4 Ask the students to come to the board. Each student writes their name next to the name of one of the native speakers.

5 Explain that each student must get into a conversation with the native speaker and tell them their biography before the next class.

6 Next time the class meets, check how effectively this has been done.

VARIATION There are obviously endless variations on this theme. It works well to ask each student to tell the same thing to a different person and come back to class to compare the reactions.

COMMENTS Associating each member of the class with a particular native speaker provides an opportunity to practise a little more English and the extra thrill of having to plan how and when to talk to someone. There will inevitably be students who draw the short straw (for example, the Principal of the school)—this adds to the fun.

10 Self-improvement

There is always a balance to be struck between direct teaching and learner self-instruction. Beginners clearly require a lot of direct teaching. Yet precisely because beginners are so reliant on their teacher, their wish to be more autonomous is particularly strongly felt. Thus most adult beginners are very strongly motivated by self-study and will typically invent their own learning strategies. One very knowing learner of my acquaintance used to ring words that 'bothered' him in Italian newspapers, and then return to them later to try and puzzle them out, only resorting to a dictionary when it was absolutely necessary. It is worth fostering the beginner's wish to be autonomous.

This chapter focuses on developing learner strategies, promoting self-reliance, classroom support activities, peripheral learning, and self-study. The underlying purpose is to raise the students' awareness of how the language works and, more importantly, of how they are learning. It is necessarily orientated towards adult learners rather than child learners.

The first two activities raise the issue of learner strategy. The remaining thirteen are arranged on a cline from in-class activities started by the teacher and completed by the learner, through those that promote peripheral learning, to two or three at the end of the chapter that are genuine out-of-class, self-instruction activities.

10.1 Learning on the go

LEVEL   2–4; (children and) adults

TIME   40 minutes

LANGUAGE   Everyday contexts: driving to work, in the bath

PREPARATION   Think up 15 to 20 everyday situations which might be combined with learning a language. Good situations include driving to work, walking to work, in a restaurant, on a train, on a plane, in bed, in the cinema, cooking, in the bath, watching television, listening to music, reading the newspaper, on holiday.

PROCEDURE

1 Tell the students that you will dictate 15 everyday contexts to them at the rate of one every forty seconds. As they hear each one, they should write down one good way of learning English in this situation. For example, if you dictate 'Driving to work', a student might write down 'Listening to a cassette'. They should write their ideas down in English if possible, but allow the use of the mother tongue if this is easier.

2 After the dictation, ask the class for suggestions for each situation. Tell the students to write down any good ideas they hear from classmates which they might try themselves.

3 Ask each student to think seriously about the lists they have made and try to rank the ideas, with the ones they are likeliest to try at the top.

COMMENTS

Successful learners have to make real changes in their lifestyle to learn a language properly and reasonably rapidly. This activity encourages them to begin the process of thinking about the changes in lifestyle that will be necessary.

10.2 Sharing learning strategies

LEVEL

3–4; adults

TIME

30 minutes +

LANGUAGE

'Yes/no' questions; language learnt through self-study

PROCEDURE

1 Ask the students to write down in either English or their mother tongue one strategy they have for learning English.

2 Ask for a volunteer and tell the other students to try and guess their classmate's strategy by asking 'yes/no' questions, such as 'Is it reading?', 'Do you use a dictionary?', 'Do you do it in bed?'

3 When everyone has been questioned, ask each student to write down two English words, phrases, or sentences that they have learnt by the strategy they wrote down at Step 1.

4 Allow 5 to 10 minutes for the students to work in small groups and tell each other what they have learnt through their particular strategy.

10.3 Asking real questions, giving real answers

LEVEL   2–4; children and adults

TIME   30 minutes

LANGUAGE   Question and answer frames such as 'Why . . .?' 'Because . . .'

PROCEDURE   1 Suggest a number of question and answer frames to the students. Good examples include

– Why . . .? Because . . .
– When . . .? When/Last/In . . .
– Who . . .? [Name]/I . . .
– How . . .? By . . .
– Where . . .? In . . .

2 Ask each student to take a sheet of paper and write down a question that they would like answered and give the first word of the expected answer. For example:

Why did Charles marry Di?
Because . . .

3 Ask the students to leave their questions on their desks and circulate, trying to provide answers to classmates' questions. They should only write an answer when they genuinely think they are being informative and when that answer has not already been suggested by someone else.

VARIATION   If it is difficult to have students moving round the classroom, at Step 3 pass the question sheets round the class.

COMMENTS   It is important to stress at Step 1 that these should be serious questions about topics that genuinely intrigue the student. If they then receive meaningful answers, this helps to give the students the feeling that they are getting somewhere through English, and learning strategies that will make them more self-reliant.

10.4 Talking to oneself in English

LEVEL

1–4; children and adults; small classes (or larger classes divided into smaller groups)

TIME

30 minutes

LANGUAGE

Names of countries, illnesses, injuries

PREPARATION

Make a big wall chart in the form of a graph. Mark in the names of all the class members on the vertical axis and the years from birth (for children) or from the age of 16 (for adults) on the horizontal axis. Display this on the wall.

PROCEDURE

For classes where the students have all travelled to other countries, ask each student to write in the names of any countries visited in the appropriate years. For classes where the students have not travelled, ask each student to write in any illnesses or injuries suffered in the appropriate years. As they do this, they should talk aloud to themselves in English about what they are writing.

Name	0	1	2	3	4	5	6	7	8	9	10	11	12	13	14	15	16
Belma				chicken pox													
Winnie		mumps															
Celeste																	
Zofia																	
Rani					mumps												Append-icitis
Marianna								chicken pox									
Csilla																	
Aprieste									tonsils out				flu				
Agnieszka				measles													
Lulu																	
Lisa									broken leg								

2 Use this as the basis for bringing the students together in small groups to discuss common experiences.

VARIATION 1

Other good topics for class wall-charts of this type include notable achievements, major changes in lifestyle, new jobs, changes of address, new friends.

VARIATION 2

Ask each student to make an individual graph in which they plot the fluctuations in their disposable wealth by year, talking aloud to themselves as they do this. Later they explain their graph to a neighbour. Other good topics that can be plotted on a graph include happiness, fitness, emotional relationships, frustration.

COMMENTS

1 This activity enables the students to get to know more about each other and thus promotes a trusting atmosphere in the classroom. It is a good idea to leave the graphs or wall charts on display for a while.

2 Encouraging the students to mutter to themselves in English as they work is also very important. This is a prelude to thinking in the target language.

3 But because the students are all working on a single graph on the wall, it will only work with small classes or groups.

10.5 Diary ideas

LEVEL

1–4; adults and children

MATERIALS

Each student will need an exercise book to use as a diary

LANGUAGE

Diary entries

Diaries that record language learning progress

Get the students to use formulas like

– today/this week I learnt . . .
– today I . . . in English

or to use headings like 'Me and English' or 'English and Me'. The most important things are for the diary to be truthful and develop its own form. There is nothing wrong with making the same entry day after day.

Mother-tongue diaries

These can take several forms, such as

– describing what the student hopes to learn next in English
– describing the time spent learning English words and phrases and the way it felt (encourage language mixing rather than translation)
– being about teacher(s), lesson(s), and classmates.

Fictional diaries

The students keep fictional diaries over a limited period (one or two weeks are best), imagining themselves staying with an English-speaking or a British/American family. Allow language mixing if writing everything in English is too challenging.

Conversations with the diary

The students write a 'Dear Diary' letter about their English on Days 1, 3, and 5, and on Days 2, 4, and 6 their diary replies to them.

COMMENTS

The point of a diary is that it should be a private, developing record of progress being made. Because it is private, there is no reason why it should not be written partly in the mother tongue. The diary is bound to find its own form and each student will work in their own way. This means that as the teacher you need to stand well back from the diary and not expect to read it—only to act as a sounding-board for language questions.

10.6 Scrapbook ideas

LEVEL

1–4; adults and children

MATERIALS

A scrapbook for each student; magazines, postcards, etc.

Scrapbook ideas

It is a good idea to put regular class time aside for the students to add to their scrapbooks while you are available to give advice and assistance. The following make good ongoing scrapbook activities:

– each page of the scrapbook is dedicated to a different person. Encourage the students to choose a mixture of people they know personally and people they have never met. Encourage them to give their chosen people news and views as presents. These presents can include printed materials from newspapers and magazines as well as news of their own language learning progress
– allocate 10 pages to 10 significant years in the student's life
– use two or three pages for names (of people in the news or known to them, and/or of places visited) each followed by a single sentence.

A diary or scrapbook week

A theme for each day works well, with the students encouraged to write down 'scraps' of information that may be more meaningful to them than to others. Good themes include making money, being careful with money, learning English, relaxing, enjoying the weekend, resolutions that they hope to effect, having a good day, being happy.

Focus on English week

An idea a day, such as

- soliciting contributions from native speakers written in their own hand
- pictures of Britain or another English-speaking country with appropriate captions
- samples of English found in the local environment, including advertisements, notices, menus
- pictures and stories about selected people (politicians, entertainers, royals), or topics (sport, entertainment, politics), or English-speaking countries (Australia, USA), all from mother-tongue sources, with English commentaries and one-liners supplied by the students
- pictures of the student's own town with simple English commentaries prepared for an English-speaking visitor or penfriend
- anything about their own country or nationals from English-speaking countries' newspapers and magazines (when available).

Memory Lane 1

Set aside part of the scrapbook for target-language or target-culture experiences which are triggered by key words the students meet in class, such as 'chips' or 'toast'. The scrapbook should make a connection between the key word and the memory of a visit to an English-speaking country, an encounter with a native speaker of English, British or American eating experiences, British or American television or films, etc.

Memory Lane 2

Set aside part of the scrapbook for representations of the student's own life in English. This might include family trees with glosses in English (for example, 'My sister is called Maria. She is younger than me.'), photographs of themselves with English captions, plans of their house or room with English glosses, descriptions of property (bicycle, car, etc.), accounts of a typical day.

COMMENTS

The point of a scrapbook is that it should be a personal memento in which pictures, drawings, and souvenirs are wrapped in language. Even the mother tongue can be wrapped in English in a scrapbook. This encourages the students to give real thought to how to design pages that have English as their frames.

10.7 Constructing one's own fidel charts

LEVEL 3–4; adults

TIME Ongoing, occasional work

MATERIALS Several large sheets of paper or card; felt pens in at least two colours

LANGUAGE Consonants where the sound–spelling correspondence breaks down

PREPARATION Fix several large sheets of card or paper to the wall.

PROCEDURE 1 Whenever the class encounters a consonant whose written representation is not predictable, write the word in which the sound occurs in the next empty space on the sheets of card on the wall. Use a black felt pen for all of the word, except the part which represents the problem sound; choose a different colour for this. So, for example, if the sound was [f] in the word 'photo', you would write 'ph' in one colour, say blue, and 'oto' in black.

2 Whenever this sound occurs again, write the word in which it occurs in the next empty space on the card, using the same colour as before for that part of the new word which contains the sound in question. So, if you came across 'cough', you would write 'cou' in black and 'gh' in blue. Each time a new word is put up, practise all the words on the wall charts containing the same sound.

```
photo   knee

cough   knit

laugh   gnat
```

VARIATION 1 As your beginners make more progress, you can start a second chart for vowels. These are much more difficult and varied.

VARIATION 2 You can also list spellings which represent non-phonetic information. For example, the sound 'b' in 'bomb' has a role in 'bombard', and if we spelt 'anxious' and 'anxiety' as they sound, something important would be lost.

VARIATION 3

Make a big alphabet chart with one simple example for each consonant. (The symbols required are b, c, ch, d, f, g, h, j, k, l, m, n, p, r, s, sh, t, th (thin), th (then), v, w, z.) Each time the class comes across a letter or a combination of letters that are not pronounced phonetically, write the word on the alphabet chart under the appropriate symbol and with the relevant letter(s) underlined.

COMMENTS

This activity is not nearly as easy to run as you might at first think. It is frequently difficult to know whether to represent one or two sounds with a single colour—'laugh' is a good example. And then what does one do with 'graph'? Quite often there will be more than one problematical sound in a single word: 'giraffe' has [dʒ] represented by 'g' and [f] represented by 'ffe'. Absolute consistency does not matter so much as picking out and drawing attention to items likely to be problematical for your students.

Acknowledgement

Although the purpose is quite different, the debt to Gattegno's Silent Way fidel charts is obvious.

10.8 Words we already know

LEVEL

2–4; adults

TIME

Day 1, 20–25 minutes; subsequent days, 5 minutes of non-class time

MATERIALS

Word cards (see Preparation)

LANGUAGE

Cognates of the mother tongue

PREPARATION

Day 1

Prepare one set of 10 cards with a different English word written on each for every 10 students in your class. The words should be words the students have already met or whose meanings they will readily guess, and they should have similar forms in their mother tongue. If the students' mother tongue is not familiar to you, it is often a good idea to use a bilingual dictionary to make sure you do not make any mistakes.

Subsequent days

Each day prepare two more word cards for every set of 10 students.

PROCEDURE

Day 1

Put the students in groups of 10 and distribute a set of cards to each group. Tell them to order the words according to their similarity to the same words in their mother tongue. Once they have ordered the words, the cards should be blu-tacked to the wall.

Subsequent days

Blu-tack the two new word cards to the wall near the list, but do not allow class time for them to be incorporated into the wall display. Let the students do this in their break time. This way you gradually allow the students to take more responsibility for their learning and neatly avoid the tricky problem of having to make decisions about the way the set of words has been ordered.

VARIATION

See 5.11, 'Recognizing familiar words', for a variation suitable for learners with Greek and Cyrillic mother-tongue writing systems.

COMMENTS

1 As your students learn more (about) English, they will begin to revise their original opinions as to the best order for the words without relying on your advice.

2 If you have a class with speakers of different Indo-European languages, each language group can order a set of words. This provides an interesting opportunity for the students to learn more about each others' languages.

10.9 You can't say this in English

LEVEL

3–4; adults (and children)

LANGUAGE

Non-possible English structures

PREPARATION

Prepare a big sheet headed 'You can't say this in English' and display it on the wall.

PROCEDURE

1 Whenever a student comes up with a plausible but non-possible English structure, write it up on the 'You can't say this in English' sheet. It is important that you only write up plausible but non-possible structures such as '*I live at London'. Where appropriate, also indicate the correct structure on the sheet. Try to avoid making any comment when you write up one of these structures.

2 Occasionally, add something of your own such as 'On Tuesday, you can't say "On Wednesday", you must say "Tomorrow".' Again, do not comment—in any case there is no need with this example, which is universal.

COMMENTS	The whole point of peripheral learning is that the students should teach themselves. As little teacher comment as possible is therefore best.

10.10 Alphabet stories

LEVEL	3–4; adults and children
TIME	Occasional non-class time
MATERIALS	Alphabet chart (see Preparation)
LANGUAGE	A story invented by the students
PREPARATION	Prepare an alphabet chart which runs round the wall of the classroom and allows space after each letter for a word to be written in. Each letter should be repeated four times so that your chart will look like this:

a	b	c	d	
a	b	c	d	
a	b	c	d	
a	b	c	d	etc.

PROCEDURE	Encourage the students to think of words beginning with the letters in such a way as to make a continuous story. This should be done outside class time, i.e. in break times and before the beginning of class. You can set an example by beginning one of the stories with 'A big cat . . .' if you like.
VARIATION 1	With small groups, allow each student to produce their own alphabet chart with the 26 letters ordered in any way they wish. Allow five minutes a day for the students to add words to any chart but their own. The winning chart is the one that is completed first.
VARIATION 2	You can pep this activity up a bit by writing in one or two words some way ahead of where the students have got to. This makes them consider how to complete the stories in such a way as to incorporate words that are written in already.
COMMENTS	This is an ideal peripheral learning idea because it exercises the students' minds and is not the explicit focus of anything that is being taught. The fact that some stories grind to a natural halt is instructive—do not try and salvage them.

10.11 Progressive translation

LEVEL

1–4; children and adults

TIME

30 minutes either in or out of class

LANGUAGE

Days of the week, forms of transport, sports

PROCEDURE

1 Get the students to supply categories they are interested in and would like to be able to talk about in English. Add some of your own. The categories should be written on the board. Good categories include days of the week, months, colours, forms of transport, sports they like watching or playing, the furniture in their room, the types of enterprise or institution found in a town or a high street, the contents of their handbag or wallet.

2 Ask the students to choose one or more of these categories to work on individually. Allow 20 minutes for the students to write down long lists in their mother tongue(s) of words in each category they choose. These should be words they are interested in and would like to be able to say in English. They should use a separate sheet for each category they choose.

3 Explain that as the students get to know the English equivalents for the words they have written down, they should write them beside the mother-tongue words on their lists. They may use whatever strategies they want for learning these words, from working with a dictionary to waiting until they hear the relevant words used. The important thing is that they should make this an ongoing vocabulary acquisition task over several weeks.

COMMENTS

This activity brings into focus the vocabulary that students feel they need. Since vocabulary is usually learnt in contexts, and meanings are progressively understood as the words are encountered with greater frequency, this activity helps students to know what they are looking for. Typically, a student will hear a word two or three times before turning to the dictionary and confirming that it means what they had thought it meant. This activity therefore helps students to work out the study habits that suit themselves best.

10.12 Decorating your room

LEVEL
2–4; children and adults

TIME
10–15 minutes per day out of class; occasional in-class sessions

MATERIALS
Authentic texts provided by students

LANGUAGE
Texts the students find difficult and intriguing

PROCEDURE
1 Ask each student to find an illustrated text that is aesthetically pleasing to look at and contains written English that they do not understand. Comic strips, food packaging, and advertisements are all suitable.

2 Tell the students to display their texts in their bedrooms and spend a few minutes each day trying to puzzle their meaning out—they may use dictionaries and consult friends.

3 When a student feels they have puzzled out a text, it should be brought to class and explained.

4 Encourage students to keep on collecting problem texts so that in due course several are displayed in their bedrooms. Gradually make the in-class explanations less formal—by grouping students, suggesting they share their insights at break-times, etc.

COMMENTS
In many countries, things written in English have status. For this reason, younger learners are often enthusiastic about decorating their rooms with them.

Bibliography

Ball, W. 1986. 'Writing English script: an overlooked skill.'
ELT Journal 40/4: 291–8.

Candlin, C. 1984. 'Syllabus design as a critical process' in C. J.
Brumfit (ed.) *General English Syllabus Design*. Oxford:
Pergamon.

Ellis, G. and **B. Sinclair.** 1989. *Learning to Learn English*.
Cambridge: Cambridge University Press.

Gass, S. M. and **J. Schachter** (eds.). 1989. *Linguistic
Perspectives on Second Language Acquisition*. Cambridge:
Cambridge University Press.

Goodman, K. S. 1967. 'Reading: a psycholinguistic guessing
game' in *Journal of the Reading Specialist* 6/1: 126–35.
Reprinted in H. Singer and R. Ruddell (eds.). 1986 (3rd edn):
Theoretical Models and Processes of Reading. Hillsdale, NJ:
Laurence Erlbaum Associates.

Grundy, P. 1993. *Resource Books for Teachers: Newspapers*.
Oxford: Oxford University Press.

Hardisty, D. and **S. Windeatt.** 1989. *Resource Books for
Teachers: CALL*. Oxford: Oxford University Press.

Hargreaves, R. 1976. *Mr Noisy*. London: Thurman Publishing.

Krashen, S. D. 1981. *Second Language Acquisition and Second
Language Learning*. Oxford: Pergamon.

Stevick, E. W. 1986. *Images and Options in the Language
Classroom*. Cambridge: Cambridge University Press.

Svanes, B. 1987. 'Motivation and cultural distance in second
language acquisition.' *Language Learning* 37/3: 341–59.

Svanes, B. 1988. 'Attitude and cultural distance in second
language acquisition.' *Applied Linguistics* 9/4: 357–73.

Van Ek, J. A. 1975. *Systems Development in Adult Language
Learning: the Threshold Level*. Strasbourg: Council of Europe.

White, I. D. 1988. 'Ethnocentric, Graphological and Linguistic
Assumptions in English Language Teaching.' University of
Durham: unpublished MA dissertation.

Indexes

Activity types

Acquiring vocabulary 2.6, 2.8, 4.3, 5.10, 6.2, 6.3, 6.5, 6.8, 6.11, 6.13, 7.13
Alphabet work 4.6, 8.2, 10.10
Autobiography 3.5, 3.10, 5.3, 6.6, 7.2, 8.3, 9.7
Commentaries 7.1
Creating stories 8.7, 8.8, 10.10
Cultural focus 2.2, 2.3, 2.4, 3.13, 5.3
Listening comprehension 7.13
Listing achievements 3.15
Matching 3.11, 3.13, 3.14, 4.6, 5.8, 5.11, 6.2, 6.8, 6.12, 7.8, 7.14, 8.3, 8.4
Questionnaire 7.5
Role play 6.4
Roman script
   production 5.1, 5.2, 5.3, 5.4, 5.5, 5.6, 5.7, 5.9
   recognition 5.8, 5.10, 5.11
Surveys 7.6
Testing 7.4
Text work 7.7, 7.8, 7.11, 7.12, 7.16, 8.1
Translating 2.2, 4.7, 5.9, 10.5, 10.11
Useful tasks 9.4
Visuals 2.5

Language awareness

Cognates 5.11, 10.8
International English 2.2
Lip reading 7.14, 7.15
Loan words 2.1
Manner and place of articulation 5.8
Non-possible sentences 10.9
One-word sentences 9.5
Phonetic minimal pairs 4.7
Polysyllabic stress 4.8
Possible words 5.4, 6.10
Reduced vowels 2.9, 4.8
Semantic fields 6.1
Sound–spelling correspondence 10.7
Stress assignment 4.9, 4.11
Word boundaries 4.10, 4.11
Word combination 5.5

Language functions

Asking and answering 3.4, 4.5, 6.9, 9.2, 10.3
Describing a room 7.13
Everyday phrases 9.1
Finding out about others 7.5
Likes 2.1, 6.5
Presenting self 2.9, 2.10, 3.1, 5.2, 9.2, 9.7
Talking about self 3.2, 3.7, 3.9, 3.12, 4.2, 10.4
Telling the time 3.6, 3.7
Topic and comment 4.4
Using functional English 9.6
Writing holiday postcards 7.9

Language structures

Adjectives 3.7, 8.1
Adverbs 8.1, 8.5, 8.10
Conjunctions 8.5
Demonstratives 2.3
Plurals 3.2
Prepositions 4.1, 7.13
Present perfect 4.2, 4.3, 4.5
Present progressive 4.1, 7.1
Superlatives 4.5
Temporal clauses 3.10
Wh- **questions** 3.4, 3.14, 6.11, 7.4, 7.6, 10.3
Yes/no questions 6.9, 7.6